LA COMIDA DEL BARRIO

LA COMIDA DEL BARRIO

AARÓN **SANCHEZ**

photographs by emmanuel bastien

latin-american cooking in the U.S.A.

text with joann cianciulli

CLARKSON POTTER/PUBLISHERS
NEW YORK

Published by Clarkson Potter/Publishers, New York,
New York.
Member of the Crown Publishing Group, a division of
Random House, Inc.
www.randomhouse.com

CLARKSON N. POTTER is a trademark and POTTER and
colophon are registered trademarks of Random House, Inc.

Printed in the United States of America

Design by Jan Derevjanik

Library of Congress Cataloging-in-Publication Data
Sanchez, Aarón.
   La comida del barrio : Latin-American cooking in
the U.S.A. / Aarón Sanchez ; photographs by
Emmanuel Bastien.
      p.   cm.
Includes index.
1. Cookery, Latin American. I. Title.
TX716.A1 S26   2003
641.598—dc21   2002008501

ISBN 0-609-61075-9

10 9 8 7 6 5 4 3 2 1

First Edition

CONTENTS

¿POR QUÉ EL BARRIO?

This book is not about "authentic" regional dishes from one or another village in Mexico or Cuba or Brazil. This book is about Latin-*American* food, the cuisine of the barrio. The barrio is not a monolithic slum, not a segregated ghetto. The barrio is a vibrant neighborhood, often composed of people from vastly diverse cultures: Cubans, Dominicans, Panamanians, and other African-descendant Caribbeans; Puerto Ricans and similarly mixed-European islanders; Mexicans from the Sonoran desert, the highlands of Chiapas, or the jungles of the Yucatán; Guatemalans, Nicaraguans, Salvadorans, Hondurans, and other Central Americans of primarily indigenous descent; and South Americans as diverse as Peruvian Incas and Portuguese-speaking Brazilians.

Most cookbooks about this food strive for international authenticity, whether their authors are Latin-American or simply lovers of the food; the aim has been to re-create the traditional overseas experience here in America, to import the food and life of a foreign land to an American audience that's hungry for new tastes and cultural experiences. In fact, the same is true for most international cookbooks, whether Italian or French or Southeast Asian.

But these new cultural experiences don't always have to be imported from abroad; they can be imported from uptown. Or downtown. Or across the river, or the other side of the tracks. Hispanics are the largest "minority" in the United States—32 million people, or 12 percent of the population; there are more Latin-Americans in the States than there are residents of Canada. This immense population—the fastest-growing segment of American demographics—has created a new culture, in new neighborhoods. And this new culture is not an exact transplant of the motherland's, just as Little Italy is not Palermo, and Chinatown is not Taipei. In the crossing to the United States, many things change. Not the least of which is the food. Ingredients here are different, with different availabilities; cooking methods and tools are different; the surrounding culture is different; and the people who've chosen to emigrate, for whatever reason, are different.

Just as ethnic neighborhoods like New York's Little Italy and Chinatown gave rise to new interpretations of the original cuisines, so too has the barrio. The chapters that follow will introduce home cooks to the range of the barrio's rich culinary geography and its key ingredients and cooking techniques, and will provide recipes for typical dishes. While some of these dishes are identical to the ones made back in the homeland, many are different. But this book will not focus on atmospheric romance—I will not discuss the beautiful old *campesinas* cooking their *birilla* in a homemade ceramic pot over an open flame in a remote mountain village; I will not wax poetic about the joys of burying a suckling pig with hot rocks under the sand of the Yucatán. Those texts and recipes are about another place, and another time.

This book is about the here and now—the creative, delicious cuisine that has roots in Latin America but was born and grew up in the United States. This book is filled with recipes whose ingredients are available in your local supermarket or corner bodega; no mail-ordering is necessary to achieve the most true-to-the-original *mole poblano*. This book is about real food that real people can—and do—cook and eat every day and night, on a reasonable budget; we are not combining fifteen-dollar-per-pound rack of lamb with twenty hard-to-find ingredients. This book is about *real* Latin-American food, not some fancy chef's interpretation of what Latin-American-inflected food could be with European techniques and an unlimited budget. That chef isn't me.

I have been especially lucky in my career as a chef. To begin with, I was born the son of one of the culinary pioneers who brought authentic Mexican cooking to the United States, first in El Paso, then in New York City. So I grew up in restaurants, working and playing and just living in them. I learned an immense amount during a *stage*—a sort of apprentice job—with the world-renowned chef Paul Prudhomme and during my studies at one of the premier culinary schools in the world, Johnson & Wales. I was fortunate to find grueling, rewarding jobs at top-flight restaurants: Patria, one of the most ambitious Latin-American restaurants in the United States, run by the groundbreaking chef (and cookbook author) Douglas Rodriguez, where I learned the value—and challenges—of creative experimentation; the lively New York hot spots Erizo Latino and L-Ray; the San Francisco destination Rose Pistola; and then Isla, back in New York City, where I designed the menu and ran the kitchen. And two years ago, I found a great partner and a great space in a great neighborhood and became chef-owner at Paladar, on New York City's Lower East Side; we've been lucky enough to be both well-reviewed by the press and well-received by diners. The restaurant world has treated me well.

My role as one of the hosts of Food Network's *Melting Pot* has also afforded me great opportunities—to travel, to meet other chefs (both professionals and home cooks), and to reach millions of food lovers who will never be able to visit my restaurant. Plus, it's a blast to be on television. Though my professional experiences led to my writing this cookbook, it is my personal heritage and life that this book reflects—a Latin-American one, not just a Latin one or an American one. I wanted the food to be delicious, of course, but not fussy restaurant food, nor the "homeland" food that so few people truly want to cook. I wanted the book to teach something interesting, and not to prove what a creative chef I am. (Who cares?) One obvious subject presented itself—the foods of the American barrios, which encompass everything I love most about Latin-American culture.

So I set out to research—I scoured the barrios, talked to the cooks, the people at market stands, the bodega owners, the guys playing cards on the sidewalk. I talked to chefs and friends across the country. I ate thousands of tacos, hundreds of tamales. I looked for the dishes that were most typical of the neighborhoods—the favorite Puerto Rican dishes from the Bronx, the favorite Cuban dishes from Miami's Little Havana, the favorite Mexican dishes from the Mission District in San Francisco. I made sure the recipes I collected were delicious, but also accessible.

And I wanted them to reflect a crucial aspect of Latin-American eating: the importance of the *type* of eating establishments, the primacy of place. American cooks may be familiar with the types of French restaurants: the most casual wine bars and cafés, the standard menus of brasseries, the specialties of mom-and-pop bistros, and the luxurious dining experience of the formal restaurants. You don't order a sandwich at a restaurant, and you don't get a cheese course at a café; you have a beer at a brasserie, not at a wine bar. If you're looking for a rustic, soul-warming stew, you go to a bistro; if you're looking for a perfectly cooked piece of fish in a classic reduction sauce, you go to a restaurant.

A similar type of division exists in Latin America—and has been transported to the United States. But because Latin Americans are less formal than the French, the emphasis is on the more casual end of things. Also, the main meal of the Latin diet is lunch, while dinner is usually simple. But whether it's breakfast, lunch, snack, drink, dinner, or dessert, there are different places for each, depending on your appetite, your schedule, and your *dinero*.

The center of Latin food life—in fact, maybe the center of Latin life, period—is the market, and in the market are the most casual eateries: the *fondas*, or market stands, run by a family, offering a few dishes daily, made fresh that day (or the night before) from what's available seasonally. This is where a sit-down lunch—albeit a quick, rustic one—is had, on a stool at a counter. The typical *fonda* dish is a big pot of something that can be made ahead and can sit for hours over a low flame, and will just get better as it sits, like soup.

Slightly less casual are *paladares*, tiny restaurants (sometimes as tiny as a single table) run out of private homes, with a very limited daily menu (sometimes as limited as a single dish) but here served on a table, not a counter. As at *fondas*, the offering is usually a large pot that improves during the day, but more substantive: stews.

For a quick lunch on-the-go or the typical light dinner, you visit a *taquería*, the Latin equivalent of a fast-food restaurant. The food is quick, cheap, and portable—a taco, a tamale, a *torta*; you can eat at a table or while walking

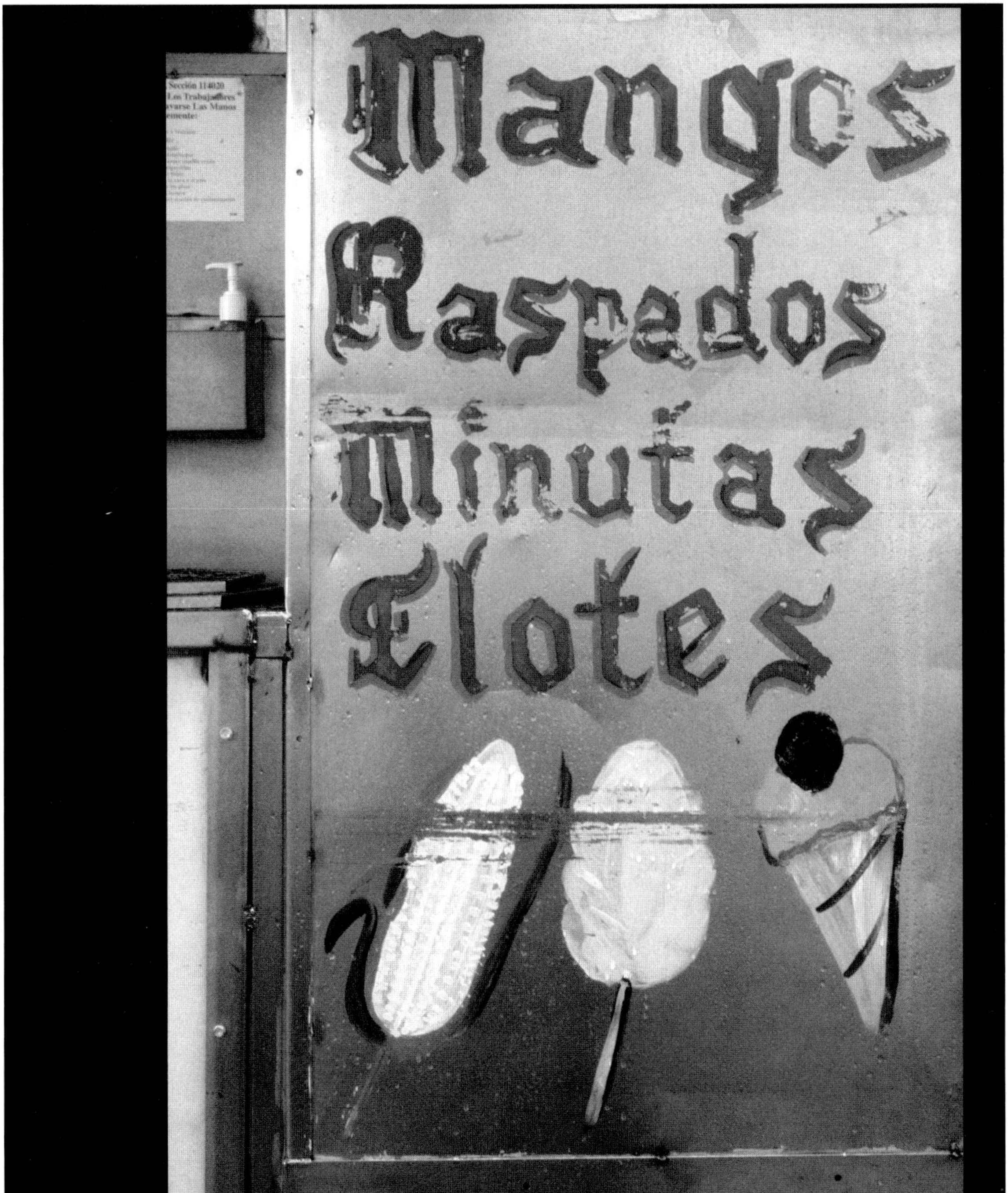
Mangos
Raspados
Minutas
Elotes

home. But unlike at typical American fast-food chains, the food doesn't arrive in the kitchen prepared, ready for a quick nuke, nor does it come from some centralized commissary-type kitchen. It may be cheap and fast, but it's fresh and delicious.

The most typical lunch is the *comida corrida,* the Latin version of the prix fixe, served at a café or *rotisería.* A set menu offers a few options of an appetizer or more frequently a soup, then a choice of two or three entrées served with rice, then a dessert—typically flan or rice pudding. In this main meal of the day, the focus is the entrée—a piece of roasted or grilled meat, often marinated and usually sauced, to provide sustenance for the afternoon ahead.

Slightly more formal are *comedores*—the equivalent is somewhere between a French brasserie and restaurant—where you order à la carte, with more ambitious offerings and a wider variety of choices. Here are more complicated, more refined dishes, from the salads to the entrées, that usually reflect a regional specialty.

Besides these types of sit-down eateries, from utterly casual to formal, there's a huge variety of other joints, and these perhaps offer an even better glimpse into the Latin-American focus on place. For example, in most of the United States, we use the word *bakery* to describe a store that sells bread, desserts, even confections. Latins don't put up with such vagueness. There's the *panadería* for breads, the *pastelería* for cakes and pastries. Not to mention the *jugoería* for juices, and even the place devoted to serving *"pollo a la brasa"*—roast chicken. Just roast chicken. No kidding.

In some incarnation, all of these establishments have made their way to the barrios. You may not find them without looking—unless, of course, you live in the barrio, in which case you know exactly where they are. But they're there: bakeries where you walk around with a metal tray and long tongs, picking and choosing from baskets of freshly baked breads; simple one-counter, six-stool storefronts for a quick, nourishing bowl of pozole; there are even tamales on the street—sold from carts similar to those that were once pushed around by Italians offering ices. On corners in the Mission, you can buy an ear of grilled corn slathered in mayonnaise, lime, and chili powder—the same street-food delicacy you find on corners in Puebla, Mexico. The woman selling the corn (for a buck apiece) is probably from Puebla. But here she is, on Mission and Twenty-sixth, doing the same thing she did three thousand miles away: selling delicious snacks to hungry people walking down the street. It's Mexico, but it's not. It's America . . . but it's not. It's the barrio.

This book represents a people, and a place—the people from a few dozen countries who have come to this place, the United States, to make a new home but to maintain ties to the old one, including the food and where it's served. And so the recipes are organized along the lines of place—by the type of eating establishments explained above, instead of by main ingredient or the course of the meal. This is how we think about food.

I hope this book opens a new door for readers, one that leads them to hop on the subway to Spanish Harlem or the Mission instead of a flight to Oaxaca or Mexico City. Or to stop into the corner bodega for some plantains and sour oranges, instead of another gourmet shop for semi-boned quail. To embrace something that's exotic, but not foreign; to take an adventure in the backyard, instead of in the other hemisphere.

To explore the barrio.

TAQUITOS DE
BARBACOA

{the market stand: soups}

TACOS
DE MACIZA
$ 4.

SURTIDA· RES

$3.50 $3.50

Se Solicita
Empleada
V

CALDO GALLEGO
{galician-style soup}

SOPA DE FRIJOLES NEGROS
{black bean soup}

CALDO DE RES
{beef soup}

CHUPE DE CAMARONES
{shrimp chowder}

SOPA DE ALBÓNDIGAS
{meatball soup}

SOPA DE PLÁTANOS
{plantain soup}

MENUDO
{tripe and hominy soup}

SOPA DE CALABAZA
{pumpkin soup}

SOPA DE TORTILLA
{tortilla soup}

POZOLE VERDE
{green hominy soup}

SOPA DE CHAYOTE
{chayote soup}

IN MOST OF LATIN AMERICA, the market is the

center of life, whether it's in a tiny village that hosts a traveling market once a week or a huge city with several permanent structures set in different neighborhoods. The village markets are usually open-air affairs, with vendors traveling from farms in the surrounding area to sell produce and livestock, and from nearby cities to sell clothing, tools, and other packaged goods. These vendors travel almost every day of the week, moving from village to village—Atitlán on Tuesdays, Monte Albán on Wednesdays, every week, often for their whole lives.

In larger towns and cities, the market is more permanent. It's usually housed in a huge building that takes up a full city block, and is generally just one story but with an immensely high ceiling—the feeling is of an airplane hangar. It's divided up into scores or hundreds of stalls, and these stalls are arranged along aisles—like a trade show in a convention center. Different parts of the market are devoted to different types of products—there are separate areas for clothing, for sandals, for automotive supplies, for music, for toys; on another side of the market, there are areas for vegetables and fruits, for spices and chiles, for butchers (the most pungent area); and then there's the area for eating at *fondas,* or market stands.

The *fonda* area of the market has running water and gas lines, and each stand is set up the same way: fronting the aisle is a counter, with anywhere from four to a dozen seats; right behind the counter there's usually a griddle and cutting board, tended by the servers; behind the servers are range-tops that keep the food hot; and then there's usually a wall, behind which is the full kitchen where the food is prepared. A *fonda* is usually a family affair, with a parent or two cooking, and kids serving and cleaning. Despite the small size and limited resources of the space, these are not transient operations: A family may run a given *fonda* for generations, and they decorate it lovingly with Virgin Mary statues, homemade paper decorations, oilcloth tablecloths for the counters, and pretty bowls that contain garnishes like pickled jalapeños, chiles in vinegar, chopped white onion, cilantro, and a few salsas.

Here is where working people get lunch; you sit down at the counter and immediately order one of a few daily specials, and your bowl arrives within seconds. You eat, leave a few coins on the counter, say thank you, and walk away—fifteen minutes, tops, from the time you sit down to when you leave. The usual fare is a thick, hearty, one-dish meal of soup or stew, prepared fresh each day, simmering by mid-morning, kept hot (and improving) as the day wears on. Most *fondas* are known especially for one or two dishes that they make exceptionally well, often on one or two regularly scheduled days per week. Whatever it is, it's served with tortillas in Mexico, bread elsewhere in Latin America. If there's one type of eating establishment that best represents Latin food and life, it's the *fonda.*

There's not much of a market culture in the United States—there are very few of these types of markets anywhere in the country. But that doesn't mean there aren't *fondas*—they're just not in markets. Instead, they're little storefronts, not much bigger than a good-sized magazine stand. There's usually a brightly painted metal sign announcing the name of the *fonda,* and maybe some neon lights in a plate-glass window that fronts the sidewalk, enticing you with some plates of desserts—a big vat of flan or a lemony-looking cake or snacks like *chicharrónes* (crispy fried pork skin). Inside, there's a counter with a cash register and a few stools, but no tables; behind the counter are steam tables with rice and beans, or stove-tops with simmering soups and stews; in the rear is a kitchen. It's the same setup as in the market; it's just not actually *in* the market—it's anywhere, particularly in the barrio, but also in tony neighborhoods like SoHo or Greenwich Village in New York City. (Don't believe me? When you're in New York, take a look on the south side of Fourteenth Street, just west of Seventh Avenue near the subway entrance. Never noticed that joint before, did you?)

And nearly everything else is the same—these are family businesses where working people grab a quick lunch and the ingredients come from nearby vendors (*fondas* aren't very oriented to institutional food deliveries); the daily specials are soups and stews, prepared each morning when the cook shows up at eight A.M. Here in the barrio, though, you can usually get a bit more than just a couple of daily offerings—maybe some sandwiches, maybe a roast meat, maybe a specialty like *mole poblano*. But still, the concept remains the same: A few daily dishes are put on each morning, ready for a quick dip of the ladle and a short trip to the counter.

This transplanted variation on the *fonda* reveals one of the defining elements of life in the barrio: As much as things are different here in the United States, Latins always long for a little slice of home. Whether it's the taste of the soup itself or the feel of sitting at a counter, rubbing elbows with strangers, saying hello to the same server every day, the *fonda* provides that slice. And so do the recipes in this chapter.

One of the biggest challenges to American cooks is the diversity and unfamiliarity of Latin ingredients—a challenge that's further complicated by the fact that some ingredients go by different names in different countries, or even different names for different uses. The tuber called yuca, for example, is one of the worst offenders: cassava is its African name, and in general this is the word used to describe the tuber when it's used as a commodity—to be dried, ground, and made into a flour, which is its primary role in the Afro-Caribbean-dominated Brazil. But it's called yuca when it's used as produce, boiled or fried as a side dish, or as a starch in stews.

Chilies are no picnic either. Take *ají:* the Spanish name for an Italian frying pepper, also called the *cubanella* (which is the proper, technical name of the pepper), always called simply *ají* in Cuba. But in Peru, *ají* is the general name for any spicy chile—jalapeños and serranos are both called *ají.* Then there's the matter of dried versus fresh: Every dried chile has a fresh counterpart—sometimes *with a different name.* The *ancho* chile is a dried, smoked *poblano* pepper; the *chipotle* chile is a dried, smoked jalapeño.

Still with me? There's more—the herb *culantro,* also known as *recao* (and, in Asian cooking, as saw-leaf herb), may be spelled very similarly to cilantro, but it is in fact another herb entirely. And what's commonly called taro in the United States and Asia is called *malanga* in Latin America.

So what's the solution? Get friendly with your grocer, and don't be shy about asking questions, including whether an item has another name. If there's a sign identifying a pile of root vegetables, and the name doesn't look familiar to you, inquire—persistently. You never know what you'll find.

CALDO **GALLEGO**

This dish has three major components—white beans, cooking greens, and a mixture of winter root vegetables—and the result is a nourishing soup to be sure. I don't bother to soak beans overnight like many cooks do, which I feel removes many natural nutrients that the beans possess. The cooking greens are interchangeable: mustard greens, kale, and Swiss chard are all fine options. This dish is named after a region in northwest Spain called Galicia, where the weather is very much like that in the northwest of the United States: foggy, rainy, and damp. This one-pot meal is ideal for that sort of climate. Cubans have embraced this thick hearty soup; it is featured on many menus in Miami. Sometimes at my restaurant, I like to add clams, whose interplay with chorizo adds another dimension to this straightforward classic.

SERVES 4 TO 6

1 pound dried cannellini beans, picked through and rinsed

2 bay leaves

1 tablespoon extra-virgin olive oil

1/2 pound Spanish chorizo sausage (about 2 links), cut into 1/4-inch chunks (see Note)

1 medium white onion, diced

4 garlic cloves, minced

2 medium Idaho potatoes, peeled and cut into 1/2-inch chunks

4 small turnips, peeled and cut into 1/2-inch pieces
Salt and freshly ground black pepper

1 pound collard greens, thoroughly washed and coarsely chopped

2 tablespoons chopped flat-leaf parsley

Put the beans and bay leaves in a large pot, cover with 2 quarts of cold water, and place over medium heat. Bring to a boil, reduce the heat to low, cover, and simmer for 45 minutes, then shut off the heat and let the beans sit (they will be only halfway cooked at this point).

In a large stockpot, heat the oil over a medium-high flame, add the chorizo, and cook for 5 minutes, until crispy. Add the onion and garlic to the rendered fat and cook, stirring, for 5 minutes, until the onion is translucent. Carefully pour in the beans along with their cooking liquid and bring to a gentle simmer. Add the potatoes and turnips and cook for 20 minutes, until tender. Season with salt and pepper to taste. Add the collard greens and cook for 15 minutes more, until the greens have thoroughly softened. Garnish with parsley and serve immediately.

SPANISH CHORIZO AND LINGUIÇA

A hard, cured pork sausage. The links are rusty-red because the ground pork is well seasoned with *pimentón* (aka hot paprika). These sausages are fatty and flavorful, which makes their juices ideal for sautéing vegetables. Chorizo is often sold in vacuum-sealed packages or in links at the deli counter.

Linguiça is a heavily flavored Portuguese sausage that is often used in Brazilian cooking. It is thinner and spicier than Spanish chorizo.

SOPA DE **FRIJOLES NEGROS**

Every region of Latin America has its own version of black bean soup, some simmered with ham hock, some with chorizo. I favor this one in particular because it is completely vegetarian. Black bean soup can be garnished with almost anything from red onions to *queso*. My former employer Fernando Saralegui, who is of Cuban descent, told me his family would garnish their version with sugar and balsamic vinegar. I like to top mine with my favorite "go-to" herb, cilantro.

SERVES 4 TO 6

1	pound dried black turtle beans, picked through and rinsed
2	bay leaves
1	tablespoon dried Mexican oregano (see Note, page 73)
1¼	cups extra-virgin olive oil
1	medium white onion, coarsely chopped
1	*cubanella* or green bell pepper, cored and coarsely chopped (see Note, page 43)
1	red bell pepper, cored and coarsely chopped
8	garlic cloves, minced
1	teaspoon ground cumin
1	teaspoon ground coriander
1	teaspoon cayenne
1	teaspoon ground cinnamon, preferably Mexican *canela* (see Note)
	Salt and freshly ground black pepper
½	cup chopped cilantro, for garnish

Put the beans, bay leaves, and oregano in a large pot, cover with 3 quarts of cold water, and place over medium heat. Cover and cook the beans for 1 hour, then remove from the heat.

Meanwhile, make a *sofrito*: Coat a large skillet with ¼ cup of the oil and place over medium-low heat. When the oil begins to smoke, add the onion, peppers, and half of the garlic. Cook and stir for 10 minutes, until the vegetables have softened; don't let them brown. Transfer to a blender and purée until smooth (if necessary, add a little water to help get it going). Add the purée to the beans.

Put the skillet back on the heat and add the remaining 1 cup of oil. Add the remaining garlic and cook for 5 minutes, until lightly golden. Add the garlic-oil to the pot of beans.

Place a small dry skillet over medium-low heat, add the cumin, coriander, cayenne, and *canela*, and toast for 1 minute, until fragrant, shaking the pan so they don't scorch. Add the toasted spices to the pot.

Continue to simmer the soup for 30 to 45 minutes, until thick enough to coat the back of a spoon. Season with salt and pepper to taste. Garnish with chopped cilantro before serving.

CANELA

Also called Ceylon; the inner bark of the tropical laurel tree. The cinnamon in Mexico is flesh-colored and sold ground into powder or in whole quills, ranging from 6 inches to 1 foot long. The flavor is mild and sweet, without the astringent burn associated with powdered cinnamon (cassia). In the Latin household, *canela* is used in both sweet and savory dishes. If you must, substitute powdered cinnamon, but the dish will not be nearly as good or complex.

THE ZÓCALO

In many Latin countries, but particularly in Mexico, nearly every village, town, or city is centered around a town square, the *zócalo*. Most *zócalos* are a block or two square, with paths around the perimeter, and paths leading from each corner to the center. In the center is a band shell, and bands actually play in them, almost every Saturday night and on other nights for festivals (of which there seem to be one every week) commemorating a saint, a momentous day in national history, or nearly anything. We love festivals.

The *zócalo* is a leafy garden—this isn't a park in which to play on expanses of grass—carefully tended and regularly cleaned. The trees are old and tall, and you can often make your way to the *zócalo* simply by looking to the sky for a big clump of tall trees. On one side of the square, there's always a church—the Spanish Catholic influence tends to dominate the town in every way, including physically; the church is often the tallest building in town, and almost always the tallest building in its immediate vicinity. The other sides of the *zócalo* are usually surrounded by old, low buildings with porticos, under which are cafés and shops. From late afternoon to late at night, the cafés are packed with a mixture of tourists and locals, sipping coffee or beer, eating pastries or light suppers, and watching the town go by. And the *zócalo* itself is also packed, and everybody's eating and drinking from street vendors, sitting around on benches, and watching the town go by.

CALDO DE **RES**

It is not unusual to see people in the *fondas* having this popular beef stew. An assortment of vegetables often appears in adaptations, such as cabbage and chayote, but I prefer to keep it clean and simple—a meat-and-potatoes meal, with garnishes providing more identity. The most important step is seasoning and browning the shanks, which develops a rich brown color and adds a ton of flavor.

SERVES 4

- 4 bone-in beef shanks (about 3 pounds)
- 2 tablespoons salt
- 2 tablespoons freshly ground black pepper
- 2 tablespoons lard (page 224)
- 1 medium white onion, chopped
- 1 15-ounce can diced tomatoes
- 1 gallon Beef Stock (page 230)
- 2 ears fresh corn, husked and cut into ½-inch slices
- 2 carrots, chopped
- 8 red new potatoes, halved
- ½ medium white onion, finely diced, for garnish
- ¼ cup finely chopped cilantro, for garnish
- 1 tablespoon dried Mexican oregano, for garnish (see Note, page 73)
- ¼ cup sliced, pickled jalapeños, for garnish (see Note, page 139)

Season the beef shanks generously with the salt and pepper. Heat the lard in a large Dutch oven or other heavy-bottomed pot over a medium flame. When the lard is smoking and rippling, add the beef. Sear the shanks, turning carefully with tongs, so all sides are a brown caramel color (do this in batches if the shanks are big and look crowded in the pot). Remove to a platter.

Add the onion and tomatoes to the drippings, stirring to scrape up the flavor in the bottom of the pot. Add the meat and stock, and cover. Simmer over medium-low heat for 1½ hours, until the meat is falling off the bone.

Add the corn, carrots, and potatoes. Cover and continue to cook for 15 to 20 minutes, until the vegetables are tender. Ladle into large soup bowls and garnish with the onion, cilantro, oregano, and pickled jalapeños.

CHUPE DE **CAMARONES**

{shrimp chowder}

My good friend Alex García included this hearty Peruvian chowder on the menu at his former restaurant Erizo Latino. I've also enjoyed it at Rincón Peruano, a restaurant on Mission and Twenty-fifth Street in San Francisco. The Japanese-Peruvian chef there would use different types of local seafood as the base: crab, squid, and shrimp, depending on the season. I prefer this chowder with just a hint of evaporated milk, so the delicate flavor of the fish really shines.

SERVES 4 TO 6

2 tablespoons extra-virgin olive oil

1 medium white onion, diced

2 carrots, diced

1 celery stalk, diced

1 cup dry white wine, such as sauvignon blanc

2 quarts Shrimp Stock (page 229) or canned vegetable broth

2 medium Idaho potatoes, peeled and diced

2 tablespoons *ají amarillo* paste (see Note)

3/4 cup evaporated milk

16 medium shrimp (about 1 pound), peeled and deveined with tails on

1/2 cup pearl onions, peeled (see Note), or cocktail onions

1/2 cup frozen or fresh sweet green peas (see Note)
Salt and freshly ground black pepper

2 hard-boiled eggs, chopped, for garnish

1/4 cup chopped cilantro, for garnish

Place a large stockpot over medium heat and pour in the oil. When the oil begins to smoke, add the onion, carrots, and celery. Cook and stir for 10 minutes, until the vegetables have softened; don't let them brown. Pour in the wine and reduce by half.

Pour in the stock and bring up to a simmer. Add the potatoes and *ají amarillo* paste and simmer for 20 minutes, until the potatoes are tender. Add the evaporated milk, shrimp, pearl onions, and peas. Cook until the shrimp are firm and pink, about 5 minutes. Season with salt and pepper to taste. Garnish each bowl of chowder with chopped egg and cilantro.

AJÍ AMARILLO

A sunset-yellow chili from Peru that is somewhat banana-shaped. It is the most common of all Peruvian chiles, with a subtle flavor, acidic heat, and a color that adds a golden hue to dishes. The paste is sold in jars, or whole and packed in brine. To use, just drain, rinse, and purée in a food processor.

PEARL ONIONS

If using fresh pearl onions, blanch for 2 minutes in salted boiling water, then pinch the skins off. If using frozen pearl onions, run them under cool water for 2 minutes to thaw.

SWEET PEAS

If using fresh peas, blanch for 2 minutes in salted boiling water. If using frozen peas, run them under cool water for 2 minutes to thaw.

SOPA DE **ALBÓNDIGAS**

This soup is very popular in the American Southwest. As a youngster, I remember first sampling it in Juárez, which is just across the El Paso border. Most Latin cultures have their own version of this soup; this one is inspired by my grandmother. She always used *masa harina* instead of bread crumbs in the meatball mixture to hold them together. This recipe offers the comforting flavor of the moist meatballs in a spicy tomato broth just like my *mema* makes.

SERVES 4
MAKES 16 MEATBALLS

MEATBALLS

2	pounds ground beef
1/2	medium white onion, finely diced
2	large eggs, lightly beaten
1	tablespoon garlic powder
1	teaspoon salt
1/2	teaspoon freshly ground black pepper
2	tablespoons red wine vinegar
1/2	cup *masa harina* (see Note, page 77)

SOUP

2	tablespoons lard (page 224)
2	tablespoons all-purpose flour
2	quarts Chicken Broth (page 227)
2	scallions, white and green parts, finely chopped
4	garlic cloves, minced
1	canned green chile, chopped
2	large ripe tomatoes, chopped
1	15-ounce can tomato purée
2	medium zucchini, cut into 1/2-inch slices
	Salt and freshly ground black pepper
1/4	cup chopped mint
1/2	cup chopped cilantro

In a large mixing bowl, combine the ground beef, onion, eggs, garlic powder, salt, pepper, and vinegar. In a small bowl, whisk the *masa harina* with 1/4 cup of warm water to dissolve. Pour it into the meat mixture and gently mix with your hands to fully incorporate all the ingredients. Form Ping-Pong–size balls by rolling the mixture around in your hands. Cover and chill the meatballs so they can set and hold together better when cooked.

In a large Dutch oven or other heavy-bottomed pot, melt the lard over medium heat. Stir in the flour to make a roux. Continue to stir for about 1 minute to cook out the raw taste of the flour and to brown lightly. Slowly pour in the broth, stirring to avoid lumps. Add the scallions, garlic, chile, tomatoes, and tomato purée, and stir to incorporate. Bring to a boil, then simmer for 10 minutes to reduce the liquid slightly.

Carefully drop the meatballs into the simmering broth. Add the zucchini and cook for 15 minutes, uncovered, until the meatballs are firm and cooked through. Season with salt and pepper to taste, and shower with mint and cilantro before serving.

SOPA DE **PLÁTANOS**

In Latin folklore, a hearty plantain soup such as this has been credited with curing anything from the common cold to tuberculosis. This savory soup is commonplace in the Cuban restaurants of Miami's Calle Ocho district. The plantains add richness and a nurturing quality, but the soup doesn't weigh you down in the hot Florida sun.

SERVES 4 TO 6

¼ cup extra-virgin olive oil

1 medium white onion, coarsely chopped

2 garlic cloves, minced

1 red bell pepper, cored and coarsely chopped

1 green bell pepper, cored and coarsely chopped

1 tablespoon ground coriander

1 tablespoon ground cumin

1 teaspoon cayenne

3 green plantains, peeled and cut into 1-inch pieces (see Note, page 55)

2 quarts Chicken Broth (page 227)

Salt and freshly ground black pepper

Crema fresca or sour cream, for garnish (optional)

Place a large Dutch oven or other heavy-bottomed pot over medium heat and pour in the oil. When the oil begins to smoke, add the onion, garlic, and bell peppers. Cook and stir for 10 minutes, until the vegetables have softened; don't let them brown. Add the coriander, cumin, and cayenne, and stir constantly for 5 minutes so the spices don't burn. Add the plantains and cover with the broth. Simmer, stirring occasionally, until the plantains have become tender, about 30 minutes.

Working in batches, purée the mixture in a blender, seasoning each batch with salt and pepper to taste. Ladle the soup into bowls and garnish with a dollop of *crema fresca* if desired.

Spanish isn't just Spanish: In nearly every Spanish-speaking country, there's a different pronunciation, inflection, vocabulary, and speed—so different, in fact, that Spanish speakers from one country may barely understand those from another. Here in the barrio, native speakers can tell almost immediately—as in by the very first word that a person speaks—where someone else is from. For example, Mexican is guttural compared to other dialects, and most Puerto Ricans, Dominicans, and Caribbeans use an "l" sound to replace the "r" sound; Mexican is slow, while Caribbean is quick and singsongy.

Spanish speakers are quick to identify where one another are from based not only on language, but on looks. If you have dark skin and kinky hair, you're assumed to be Dominican; if you're short and indigenous-looking, you're presumed Mexican. And if you're relatively tall with more European features—like me—people think you're from Puerto Rico. I'm not, but I have a hard time convincing anybody of my Mexican blood.

MENUDO

Not Ricky Martin's former boy band Menudo, but the humble Mexican tripe-and-*pozole* soup, *menudo* is a particular specialty of the central coastal area of Sonora, Mexico, and San Marco, Texas, which is the host of the statewide *menudo* cook-off held every Cinco de Mayo. I think Pepe's Tamales in El Paso makes the best *menudo*, even better than their renowned tamales. My cousin's husband, Jorge, owns the restaurant chain and their outstanding soup inspires this recipe. *Menudo* is Mexico's answer to chicken soup—the home remedy for what ails you. The rich red broth that glistens with chile is believed to have medicinal properties, especially as a hangover cure after a night of wrestling with tequila. The most popular time to eat *menudo* is New Year's morning, when it is jokingly referred to as "the Breakfast of Champions."

SERVES 4 TO 6

1 pound honeycomb tripe, cut into 1-inch pieces (see Note, page 55)

1 cup freshly squeezed lemon juice (from about 10 lemons)

3 *guajillo* chiles, stemmed and seeded (see Note, page 121)

1 medium white onion, peeled and halved

4 garlic cloves, peeled

3 large ripe tomatoes, halved

¼ cup extra-virgin olive oil

1 tablespoon salt

1 tablespoon red wine vinegar

1 teaspoon ground cumin

1 gallon Chicken Broth (page 227)

1 15-ounce can hominy, drained and rinsed (see Note, page 61)

¼ cup finely chopped cilantro, for garnish

1 tablespoon dried Mexican oregano, for garnish (see Note, page 73)

1 lime, cut in wedges, for garnish

Put the tripe in a large bowl and add the lemon juice. Fill the bowl with water and let soak for 30 minutes. Remove the tripe from the lemon water, rinse, cut into 1-inch pieces, and set aside.

Bring 2 cups of water to a boil. In a dry cast-iron skillet, toast the chiles over medium-low heat for 2 minutes, until fragrant; turn them and shake the pan so they don't scorch. Put the chiles in a bowl, cover with the boiling water, and let them soak until softened and reconstituted, about 20 minutes. Put the chiles, along with 1 cup of their soaking water, in a blender and purée until completely smooth; you will have to do this in batches. Add the batches of purée to a large stockpot as you work.

Return the skillet to a medium-high flame and let it get nice and hot, a good 2 minutes. Rub the onion, garlic, and tomatoes with the oil. Lay the vegetables in the hot pan and roast, turning occasionally, until soft and well charred on all sides, about 10 minutes. Put the vegetables in a bowl to let them cool a bit, then purée until completely smooth. Add the vegetable purée to the chiles, then add the salt, vinegar, cumin, broth, hominy, and reserved tripe. Cover and simmer over medium heat for 1½ to 2 hours, stirring occasionally.

Ladle into soup bowls and garnish with the cilantro, oregano, and lime wedges.

SOPA DE **CALABAZA**

{pumpkin soup}

Calabaza is used a great deal in Latin America, much more than pumpkin is used in the States. Although *calabaza* is consumed year-round in Latin America, this soup is a nice prelude to any fall or winter meal in the colder climates. I currently have a version on the menu at my restaurant, Paladar.

SERVES 4 TO 6

1 teaspoon ground cumin

1 teaspoon ground coriander

1 teaspoon cayenne

1 teaspoon ground cinnamon, preferably Mexican *canela* (see Note, page 21)

1 1-ounce cone *piloncillo* (see Note) or 2 tablespoons dark brown sugar plus 1 tablespoon molasses

1 cup extra-virgin olive oil, plus 2 tablespoons for sautéing

1 pound *calabaza*, peeled, cleaned, and cut into ½-inch chunks (see Note, page 43)

1 medium white onion, chopped

2 garlic cloves, slivered

2 quarts Chicken Broth (page 227)
   Salt and freshly ground black pepper

½ cup heavy cream

¼ cup chopped flat-leaf parsley, for garnish

¼ cup *pepitas* (raw hulled green pumpkin seeds), roasted and salted (see Note)

Preheat the oven to 400°F.

Place a small dry skillet over medium-low heat and toast the cumin, coriander, cayenne, and *canela* for 1 minute, until fragrant, shaking the pan so they do not scorch. Put the toasted spices in a large mixing bowl. Grate the *piloncillo* with a box grater, starting with the narrow end of the cone, and add it to the spices. Add 1 cup of the oil and whisk to combine. Add the *calabaza* and toss to coat evenly in the spiced oil. Spread the *calabaza* out on a sheet pan and bake until caramelized and soft, about 30 minutes.

Coat a stockpot with the remaining 2 tablespoons of oil and place over medium heat. Add the onion and garlic and cook, stirring, for 2 minutes to soften. Add the roasted *calabaza* and broth, season with salt and pepper to taste, and simmer for 20 minutes, uncovered.

Remove from the heat. Ladle the soup in batches to a blender or food processor and purée until smooth. Return the puréed soup to the pot off the heat. Stir the cream into the hot soup to lighten it. Ladle into bowls and garnish with the chopped parsley and *pepitas*.

PILONCILLO / PANELA

A pressed, unrefined brown sugar that is often sold in small 1-ounce or larger 8-ounce cones. These "little pythons" range in color from light brown to very dark—the darker the color, the more molasses and therefore the stronger the flavor. *Piloncillo* is harder and more concentrated than regular dark brown sugar. In parts of Mexico, the sugar is formed into rounds and called *panela*. If *piloncillo* or *panela* is not available, you may substitute dark brown sugar with molasses.

To use, grate the *piloncillo* with a box grater, starting at the narrow end of the cone. If using in liquid form, chop off chunks of the cones with a sharp knife or wrap it in a towel, break it up with a meat mallet, and put the small pieces in boiling water to dissolve. Incidentally, I once chipped a food processor blade trying to grind a cone of *piloncillo*, so learn from me—don't do this!

ROASTING PEPITAS

Place a small, dry skillet over medium-low heat and toast the *pepitas* for 5 minutes, shaking the pan occasionally. Heat until the seeds are puffed and golden but not brown. Salt to taste while they are still hot.

SOPA DE **TORTILLA**

{tortilla soup}

This heartwarming soup is one of Mexico's most popular here in the States. This soup is all about the pairing of textures: the creaminess of the avocado and the crunchy bite of the tortillas. This recipe is a snap to put together and always welcome.

SERVES 4

2 tablespoons canola oil, plus more for panfrying

1 medium white onion, diced

2 garlic cloves, minced

1 jalapeño, minced

3 ripe tomatoes, chopped

1 quart Chicken Broth (page 227)
   Salt and freshly ground black pepper

4 corn tortillas, cut into 1/8-inch-thick strips

1 1/2 cups shredded cooked chicken, warm or at room temperature (page 226)

1 avocado, pitted, peeled, and diced

8 ounces Chihuahua or Jack cheese, cubed (see Note)

1/2 cup coarsely chopped cilantro, for garnish

1 lime, cut in wedges, for serving

Place a stockpot over medium heat and coat with 2 tablespoons of the oil. Add the onion, garlic, and jalapeño and cook, stirring, for 2 minutes to soften. Add the tomatoes and cook until they release their juices, about 2 minutes. Pour in the broth, season with salt and pepper to taste, and simmer for 30 minutes.

Meanwhile, heat 1 inch of oil in a skillet over a medium-high flame. When the oil begins to smoke, add the tortilla strips in batches and fry until they are crisp on all sides, about 1 minute. Remove to a paper towel–lined platter and sprinkle with salt while they are still hot.

Put a pile of shredded chicken in the bottom of four soup bowls. Ladle the hot soup over the meat. Top with the diced avocado, cheese, and fried tortilla strips. Garnish with the cilantro and lime wedges.

CHIHUAHUA

Mexico's favorite melting cheese, similar to a mild Cheddar or Jack. It is also called *queso menonita*, after the Mennonite communities of northern Mexico that first produced it. Unlike most Mexican cheeses, this mild semisoft cheese is pale yellow rather than white.

POZOLE VERDE

{green hominy soup}

This is one of the few soups you will find on *taquería* menus. Red *pozole*, which is basically *menudo* without the tripe, is often featured alongside its green cousin. Sometimes I steam some littleneck clams in this soup to kick it up a "nach'o."

SERVES 4 TO 6

1	medium white onion, peeled and halved
4	garlic cloves, peeled
20	small tomatillos, husked and rinsed
1	jalapeño
½	cup plus 2 tablespoons extra-virgin olive oil
2	*poblano* peppers (see Note, page 85)
1	cup coarsely chopped cilantro
1	teaspoon dried Mexican oregano (see Note, page 73)
1	tablespoon chopped fresh epazote or 2 tablespoons dried (see Note, page 85)
2	quarts Chicken Broth (page 227)
1	15-ounce can hominy, drained and rinsed (see Note, page 61)
	Salt and freshly ground black pepper
2	limes, cut in wedges, for garnish

Put a dry skillet over a medium-high flame and let it get nice and hot, a good 2 minutes. Rub the onion, garlic, tomatillos, and jalapeño with ½ cup of the oil. Lay the vegetables in the hot pan and roast, turning occasionally, until soft and well charred on all sides, about 10 minutes. Allow the vegetables to cool. Peel the skin from the jalapeño and remove the stem. Transfer to a blender and purée in batches until completely smooth. Put the batches of purée in a large stockpot as you work.

Rub the *poblanos* with the remaining 2 tablespoons of oil and roast on a very hot grill, over a gas flame, or under a broiler, until the skins are blistered and blackened on all sides. Put the peppers in a bowl, cover with plastic wrap, and let sweat for about 10 minutes to loosen the skins. Peel and rub off the charred skins, pull out the cores, and remove the seeds. Put the *poblanos*, along with any collected juices, in the blender and purée until smooth; add to the stockpot.

Purée the cilantro, oregano, epazote, and broth together in the blender. Add this green purée to the stockpot also. Place the pot over medium heat, add the hominy, and season with salt and pepper to taste. Stir everything together and simmer, uncovered, for 20 minutes. Serve with lime wedges.

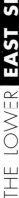

THE LOWER EAST SIDE

New York City has always been a melting pot, and the Lower East Side has always been an immigrant's neighborhood within it. Beginning in the late nineteenth century, this was a Jewish neighborhood made up of new arrivals from Eastern Europe. There are tons of synagogues, and the area around Delancey and Orchard Streets is still dominated by Jewish shopkeepers, mostly Orthodox or Hasidic, selling discount clothing and textiles. (And, oddly, some of them are native Spanish speakers, from South America.)

The Lower East Side boasts one main building type: the tenement, five or six stories high, fire escapes facing the street, jam-packed with railroad apartments—you have to walk through one room to get to another, with no space devoted to a hallway. In the old days, plumbing was tough to come by; you'll still find apartments with a bathtub in the kitchen. Apartments were crowded and amenities such as hot water and heat were rare, so the residents took refuge on the street, hanging out on stoops, setting up lawn chairs by the curb, creating a rich street culture that survives to this day.

But the neighborhood has changed—in the past decades, Latins have become the dominant immigrant population. You'll see store signs without a single word of English, you'll hear the sounds of Spanish everywhere, and you'll find plenty of places to grab a taco. Some of the slummiest tenements have given way to new construction, and most others have been renovated to modern standards.

And in the past few years, the neighborhood has seen a gentrification—cool lounges, hip boutiques carrying clothes by up-and-coming designers, antique shops, French bistros. A lot of great young chefs—great young everythings, in fact—are coming here these days, and it's a vibrant, edgy neighborhood that walks a delicate line between the immigrant past and the who-knows-what future. This is where my restaurant, Paladar, is, walking that same line.

SOPA DE **CHAYOTE**

{chayote soup}

Chayote soup is popular in Mexico and the Caribbean, and is the perfect prelude to any summer meal, served hot or cold. An added bonus is that it is vegetarian. The subtle chayote takes on other flavors beautifully, like the licorice taste of the fennel.

SERVES 4 TO 6

2 tablespoons extra-virgin olive oil

1 medium white onion, chopped

2 garlic cloves, chopped

1 jalapeño, chopped

½ fennel bulb, cored and sliced

1 teaspoon fennel seed

3 chayotes, halved, rinsed, and chopped (see Note)

1 quart canned vegetable broth

1 cup coarsely chopped cilantro

1 cup heavy cream

Salt and freshly ground black pepper

Coat a stockpot with the oil and place over medium heat. Add the onion, garlic, jalapeño, fennel, and fennel seed. Cook for 5 minutes to soften. Add the chayotes, stirring to incorporate. Pour in the broth and simmer for 20 minutes, uncovered, until the chayote is tender.

Remove from the heat. Working in batches, purée the soup and cilantro together in a blender or food processor. Return the puréed soup to the pot off the heat. Stir the cream into the hot soup to lighten it and season with salt and pepper to taste.

CHAYOTE

A member of the gourd family and a relative of zucchini; the watery and mild-tasting flesh is comparable to cucumber. It looks similar to a large light green pear, but the skin is puckered on the bottom and has grooves running down the sides. Chayote was originally cultivated as a dietary staple in Costa Rica and all over Central America by the Mayan and Aztec civilizations, but now it has transcended Latin cuisine: It is used in Cajun dishes (such as stuffed with shrimp Creole) and is grown in Louisiana, where it is called mirliton; in French cuisine, they call it *christophine;* in the Caribbean, it's *cho cho.*

To prepare chayotes, remove the waxy skin with a vegetable peeler under running water. Halve the chayote lengthwise, scoop out the soft pit with a spoon, and cut into chunks. Wash your hands to remove the sticky film.

POLLOS A LA B.B.Q.
TEL.979-0267

RESPECT
DREAM FAME
POWER

{the home-kitchen
restaurant: stews}

SANCOCHO
{root vegetable stew}

CALDO DE GARBANZOS Y PATA DE CERDO
{garbanzo and pig's feet stew}

CARNE GUISADA
{beef stew}

BIRRIA
{mariachi stew}

LENGUA ESTOFADA
{braised tongue}

CONEJO ASADO
{roasted rabbit}

CARNE MECHADA
{shredded beef}

MONDONGO
{tripe stew}

FRICASÉ DE POLLO
{chicken fricassée}

FEIJOADA COMPLETA
{brazilian cassoulet}

ESTOFADO DE RABO Y POZOLE
{braised oxtail and hominy stew}

PIPIÁN DE CHULETAS DE PUERCO
{pork chops in green chile sauce}

SOPA DE MARISCOS
{seafood stew}

THE WORD **PALADAR** has two meanings.

The literal translation, used in all Spanish-speaking countries, is *palate*. But in Cuba, it's also the name of a very special type of eating establishment—the home-kitchen restaurant, where you pay to eat in someone's home. There's usually one big table in the dining room, seating as many as fifteen people—and it's almost always fifteen strangers. No menu, of course; you just eat whatever the dish is that day, although at some places you may have as many as two or three options. Formal restaurants in Cuba are often not very good, with very few choices; if you're not eating at home, your best bet is a *paladar*. This is a very traditional eating experience, popular with locals and tourists alike. (Tourists find *paladares* just by walking down the street and saying "Yes" when asked if they're looking for a place to eat.)

The *paladar* is a distinctly Cuban institution—I know of just a few of them here in the States, and they're a closely guarded secret in the barrio. But there are variations of this concept all over Latin America—very, *very* casual little joints with food that comes straight out of a home kitchen. Everywhere, the offerings center around rustic, hearty, one-pot stews that vary throughout Latin America, served with rice and beans, tortillas, or bread to soak up the rich juices, plus plantains on the side. These are real home-cooked recipes, eaten in a home; it's just not *your* home. And it's no coincidence that the *paladar's* specialty is a stew: in one bowl, you have everything you need to nourish and satisfy.

Paladar is also the name of my restaurant in New York City. I chose the name not because we serve *paladar*-type food, but because of this sense of home: When you come to my restaurant, we hope you feel as if you've come to eat home cooking in someone's home. My home.

SANCOCHO

{root vegetable stew}

In the Latin culture, it is said of a person who has been under the sweltering sun that he is *sancochado*—blistering hot, or "stewing"—and this aptly named one-pot dish is one of Colombia's national treasures. Its identity comes from the interesting blend of different root vegetables and how each imparts a flavor and texture that enhances the end result. I make this with beef most times, but feel free to try pork or chicken for some diversity, as the meat used varies from place to place.

SERVES 8

- 2 pounds beef short ribs, trimmed of excess fat and cut into 2-inch pieces
- 3 quarts Beef Stock (page 230)
- 3 tablespoons extra-virgin olive oil
- 1 medium white onion, coarsely chopped
- 1 *cubanella* or green bell pepper, cored and coarsely chopped (see Note)
- 2 ripe tomatoes, coarsely chopped
- 6 garlic cloves, minced
- 1 pound yuca, peeled and cut into 1/2-inch chunks (see Note)
- 1 pound *calabaza*, peeled, cleaned, and cut into 1/2-inch chunks (see Note)
- 2 medium Idaho potatoes, peeled and cut into 1/2-inch chunks
- 2 ears fresh corn, husked and cut into 1-inch slices
- 2 green plantains, peeled and cut into 1/2-inch slices (see Note, page 55)
- 2 tablespoons chopped cilantro
  Salt and freshly ground black pepper

Put the ribs in a large pot, cover with the stock, and place over medium heat. Cook for 1 hour, uncovered, skimming any fat or foam that rises to the surface.

Meanwhile, make a *sofrito*: Coat a large skillet with the oil and place over medium-low heat. Add the onion, pepper, tomatoes, and half of the garlic. Cook and stir for 10 minutes, until the vegetables have softened; don't let them brown. Transfer to a blender and purée until smooth (if necessary, add a little water to help get it going). Pour the *sofrito* purée into the pot with the ribs. Add the yuca, *calabaza*, potatoes, corn, and plantains. Continue to cook for 20 minutes, until the vegetables are tender when pierced with a fork.

With a slotted spoon, fish out the plantains and place them in a large mixing bowl with the cilantro and the remaining garlic. Mash together with a potato masher. Using two spoons, carefully drop heaping tablespoonfuls of the plantain batter into the simmering soup. Poach for 5 minutes until firm. Season with salt and pepper to taste and serve.

CUBANELLA

Also referred to as an Italian frying pepper; in Cuba it is commonly called *ají*. The taste is somewhat tart and not hot at all. I like using this mild pepper because of its texture and body. If it is not available, substitute a green bell pepper, but avoid using a red one, whose sweetness will overpower the delicate flavors of the stew.

YUCA

A starchy tuber used to make tapioca. In Africa, it is known as cassava; in Latin America, it is widely referred to as yuca. Yuca root has a tough brown skin, crisp white flesh, and a buttery-sweet flavor. If it is not available, substitute a starchy variety of potato, such as Idaho or russet.

Yuca has thick barklike skin that most often comes waxed because it is very perishable, so it is important to peel it. Cut the yuca in half lengthwise, then remove the skin from each half with a sharp knife (avoid using a vegetable peeler because it is not heavy-duty enough and may break). Make sure to cut out the stringy and fibrous core.

CALABAZA

A squash grown in the Caribbean and in Central and South America; also referred to as West Indian pumpkin. In fact, *calabaza* means "pumpkin" in Spanish. But don't be fooled by the name; although it shares the same shape as a pumpkin, the skin is beige and marked with strips or blotches. The flavor is sweet and more similar to that of butternut or acorn squash than American pumpkin. You may substitute either type if *calabaza* is not available.

Because they tend to grow quite big, *calabaza* are most often sold in plastic-wrapped wedges. This is definitely a winter squash that you want to attack with a sharp serrated knife when peeling. Make sure you steady it on the counter with a towel and get a firm grip. Scoop out the seeds and strings too.

CALDO DE **GARBANZOS Y PATA DE CERDO**

{garbanzo and pig's feet stew}

I absolutely love this comfort-food dish on a very cold day with a piece of crusty bread. The stew deepens with a day under its belt, so make it in advance if you have time. The dried garbanzos act like little sponges that soak up the rich, meaty broth during the cooking process. In general, I don't like using canned beans; because they're pre-cooked, they don't absorb as much flavor.

This dish has many similarities to a Madrid-style pork stew called *cocido*, which utilizes a range of pork products such as sausage and shoulder. Very often, it is the only thing many restaurants in Madrid serve. In colonial times, this dish was adopted by Puerto Rican and Caribbean cooks. Sometimes the meat and broth are served separately.

SERVES 8

- 2 unsmoked pig's feet (about 2 pounds), halved (see Note)
- 1 pound dried garbanzo beans
- 1 tablespoon extra-virgin olive oil
- 1/2 pound Spanish chorizo sausage (about 2 links), cut into 1/4-inch slices (see Note, page 19)
- 1 medium white onion, chopped
- 2 garlic cloves, minced
- 1 red bell pepper, cored and coarsely chopped
- 1 green bell pepper, cored and coarsely chopped
- 1 jalapeño, minced
- 1/2 cup tomato paste
- 1 pound *calabaza*, peeled, cleaned, and cut into 1/2-inch chunks (see Note, page 43)
- 3 medium Idaho potatoes, peeled and cut into 1/2-inch chunks
- 1/2 head green cabbage, coarsely chopped
  Salt and freshly ground black pepper
- 2 tablespoons chopped cilantro

Put the pig's feet in a stockpot, cover with 3 quarts of water, and place over medium-low heat. Simmer, uncovered, for 1 hour, skimming any fat or foam that rises to the surface. Add the garbanzos, give it a stir, and continue to cook for another 30 minutes.

Heat the oil in a large pot over a medium-high flame. Add the chorizo and cook for 5 minutes, until crispy. Add the onion, garlic, bell peppers, and jalapeño, and cook for 10 minutes, until the vegetables are soft. Ladle out 2 cups of the garbanzo broth and reserve. Transfer the rest of the broth with the garbanzos and pig's feet into the chorizo mixture and stir together.

In a separate small bowl, combine the tomato paste and the reserved 2 cups of broth. Whisk to dilute the paste and smooth out the lumps, then add it to the pot. Now it's time to add the *calabaza*, potatoes, and cabbage. Simmer for another 20 minutes, or until tender. Season with salt and pepper to taste, and finish with the chopped cilantro.

PIG'S FEET

Benefit from a long, slow cooking process to release their natural gelatin and flavor. If pig's feet are not available, by all means use unsmoked ham hocks, which have similar flavor and body.

CARNE **GUISADA**

This dish is a perfect example of Latin cooking's magic of taking inexpensive cuts of meat and adding a variety of indigenous ingredients to create something unique and delicious. You can prepare this stew with almost any variety of beef; top round and oxtail are my personal favorites. This is standard fare at most Puerto Rican and Dominican eateries in New York City's Spanish Harlem. Mexican oregano is not something typically used in a Puerto Rican kitchen, but I think it gives a nice accent to any beef dish.

SERVES 8

½ cup extra-virgin olive oil

2 tablespoons white vinegar

1 teaspoon ground cumin

1 teaspoon ground coriander

1 teaspoon cayenne

1 tablespoon dried Mexican oregano (see Note, page 73)

3 garlic cloves, minced

2 pounds top round or chuck beef stew meat, cut into 2-inch cubes

½ cup lard (page 224)

2 *cubanella* or green bell peppers, cored and diced (see Note, page 43)

1 red bell pepper, cored and diced

2 medium white onions, chopped

1 15-ounce can tomato purée

1 quart Beef Stock (page 230)

½ pound carrots (about 3 to 4 carrots), cut into ½-inch slices

3 medium Idaho potatoes, peeled and cut into ½-inch chunks

¼ cup sliced green olives

2 tablespoons capers, drained

¼ cup raisins

1 tablespoon chopped cilantro

Salt and freshly ground black pepper

In a large bowl, combine the oil, vinegar, cumin, coriander, cayenne, oregano, and garlic. Whisk until thoroughly combined, then add the beef cubes. Mix with your hands to make sure the marinade coats the meat evenly. Let sit for 20 to 30 minutes to absorb the flavor.

In a large Dutch oven or other heavy-bottomed pot, heat the lard over a medium-high flame. When the lard is smoking and rippling, add the beef and brown it on one side for 10 minutes without stirring, so it forms a crust. Turn the beef with tongs and add the peppers and onions. Cook for 10 minutes, until the vegetables soften. Pour in the tomato purée and stock and bring to a gentle boil. Add the carrots and potatoes and simmer for 20 minutes, until tender. Add the olives, capers, raisins, and cilantro. Season with salt and pepper to taste and cook for another 10 minutes, to let the flavors marry.

BIRRIA

{mariachi stew}

This rustic dish is sold on most street corners in Mexican towns. It's particularly popular during celebrations, such as weddings and baptisms, when you need to feed a gathering of hungry people. Guadalajara, the capital of the Jalisco state of Mexico, is not only the birthplace of mariachi but also of *birria*. I like using beef ribs because the bones add deep flavor and give an unctuous feel to the broth. The special smell and taste of *birria* can make any mouth water.

SERVES 10

4 *ancho* chiles, stemmed and seeded (see Note)
1 cascabel chile, stemmed and seeded (see Note)
4 *guajillo* chiles, stemmed and seeded (see Note, page 121)
2 pounds top round or chuck beef stew meat, cut into 2-inch cubes
2 pounds beef ribs, cut into 1-inch pieces
1 medium white onion, plus more for garnish, chopped
6 garlic cloves, chopped
2 bay leaves
6 thyme sprigs
1 tablespoon dried Mexican oregano (see Note, page 73)
1 tablespoon ground cumin
   Salt and freshly ground black pepper to taste
½ cup red wine vinegar
½ cup chopped cilantro, for garnish
2 limes, cut into wedges, for serving
   Corn tortillas, for serving

Bring 2 cups of water to a boil. In a dry cast-iron skillet, toast the chiles over medium-low heat for 2 minutes, until fragrant; turn them and shake the pan so they don't scorch. Put the toasted chiles in a bowl, cover with the boiling water, and let them soak until softened and reconstituted, about 20 minutes. Put the chiles, along with their soaking water, in a blender and purée until completely smooth; you may have to do this in batches.

Put the beef cubes and ribs in a large, deep Dutch oven. Add the onion, garlic, herbs, spices, and vinegar. Then add 3 quarts of water and the chile purée. Cover and simmer over medium-low heat for 2 hours, until the meat is very tender and falling off the bone.

Remove the meat from the pot and let it cool a bit. Hand-shred the meat, return it to the pot, and discard the bones. Simmer, uncovered, for 10 minutes to reduce the liquid slightly.

Ladle the *birria* into large serving bowls and garnish with the chopped onion, cilantro, and lime. Serve with warm corn tortillas.

ANCHO CHILE

Literally translated as "wide," a brownish chile that is the dried form of the fresh poblano. It has a mild, sweet flavor and is a staple in Mexican cooking.

CASCABEL CHILE

A reddish-brown dried chile that is very hot, with a nutty flavor. Its name means "jingle bell" because the seeds rattle inside when you shake it. This small, round chile is also called *chile bola* (which means "ball") because of its shape.

LENGUA ESTOFADA

{braised tongue}

I grew up eating tongue tacos. While I loved the texture of the meat, the preparation was always a bit bland for my taste—it needed a little something extra. I love the combination of sweet and tart flavors in this dish, which really lends itself to the tongue's meaty texture. This is a common choice at many taco stands here in the States as well as all over Latin America. Cooking with cow's tongue is a prime example of how the culture doesn't let any meat go to waste, and almost anything can be wrapped in a tortilla and called a taco.

SERVES 8 TO 10

- 1 beef tongue (about 2 1/2 pounds), skin removed (see Note)
- 3 quarts Chicken Broth (page 227)
- 1 tablespoon salt
- 2 1/2 tablespoons freshly ground black pepper
- 3 garlic cloves, minced
- 1 tablespoon dried Mexican oregano (see Note, page 73)
- 1/2 teaspoon freshly grated nutmeg
- 1 tablespoon white vinegar
- 3 tablespoons extra-virgin olive oil
- 3 medium white onions, thinly sliced
- 2 cups sweet red wine, such as Madeira
- 1/2 cup pitted prunes
- 2 bay leaves
- 6 thyme sprigs, coarsely chopped
- 1 tablespoon sugar
- Cooked white rice or tortillas, for serving

In a stockpot, combine the tongue, broth, salt, and 1 1/2 teaspoons of the pepper. Simmer over medium heat, uncovered, for 2 hours, skimming any fat or foam that rises to the surface. Remove the tongue to a platter and reserve 1 quart of the cooking liquid. When the tongue is cool enough to handle, peel off the outer skin and any excess fat that might be around it to expose the flesh.

In a large mixing bowl, combine the remaining 2 tablespoons of pepper with the garlic, oregano, nutmeg, vinegar, and 2 tablespoons of the oil. Whisk until thoroughly combined, and add the tongue. Turn the tongue over to coat in the marinade, cover with plastic wrap, and stick it in the refrigerator for 2 hours to absorb the flavor.

In a large Dutch oven or other heavy-bottomed pot, heat the remaining 1 tablespoon of oil over a medium-high flame. When the oil begins to smoke, add the onions and cook, stirring, for 10 minutes, until caramelized. Pour in the red wine and simmer until reduced by half, about 5 minutes. Add the reserved quart of cooking liquid. Remove the tongue from the marinade and add it to the pan, along with the prunes, bay leaves, thyme, and sugar. Reduce the heat to low, stir everything together, and cook for 1 hour, covered. Season with salt and pepper to taste. Remove the tongue, slice it, and pour the sauce over it. Serve with white rice or tortillas.

COW'S TONGUE

A tough meat that requires a long, slow cooking process to make it tender. It is important to peel off the outer skin, which is sinewy and chewy. This also allows all those incredible flavors to permeate the meat. It is sold fresh, smoked, and pickled. Fresh tongue should be pink.

CONEJO **ASADO**

This dish uses many of the savory and sweet flavors—such as cherries, olives, and capers—that really reflect the Spanish influence in all Latin-American cooking. I personally can't think about cooking rabbit without remembering my mother's family's ranch in Chihuahua, where rabbits blanketed the countryside.

SERVES 4

1	whole rabbit (about 3 pounds), cut into 5 serving pieces
1	tablespoon salt
1½	teaspoons freshly ground black pepper
2	tablespoons extra-virgin olive oil
2	red onions, diced
3	carrots, diced
1	celery stalk, diced
3	garlic cloves, minced
½	cup red wine vinegar
1	cup dry red wine, such as Merlot
10	pimiento-stuffed green olives
2	tablespoons capers, drained
3	bay leaves
2	medium Idaho potatoes, peeled and cubed
½	cup dried cherries
1	quart Chicken Broth (page 227)

Preheat the oven to 350°F.

Season both sides of the rabbit with the salt and pepper. In a large Dutch oven or other ovenproof pot, heat the oil over a medium-high flame. When the oil just begins to smoke, add the rabbit pieces, skin-side down; you may have to work in batches. Brown for 5 minutes on each side, and then remove to a platter. Add the onions, carrots, celery, and garlic to the pan drippings, lower the heat to medium, and cook for 10 minutes, until the vegetables are caramelized. Pour in the vinegar and wine, and cook the liquid down until reduced by half, about 5 minutes. Add the olives, capers, bay leaves, potatoes, cherries, and broth and stir everything together.

Nestle the rabbit back in the pot, cover, and roast in the oven for 45 minutes to 1 hour, until the leg meat (which is the densest part) is falling off the bone. Season with salt and pepper to taste and serve.

CARNE **MECHADA**

A popular recipe all over Venezuela, whose cuisine is a blend of Spanish colonial and neighboring Caribbean Islands, this dish is typically served for brunch or lunch, with rice and beans or *arepas*, which are Venezuelan corn cakes.

SERVES 8 TO 10

1 boneless beef eye roast (4 to 5 pounds), trimmed of excess fat

1 large white onion, coarsely chopped

Juice of 2 Seville oranges (about 1/4 cup; see Note, page 83)

6 tablespoons extra-virgin olive oil

2 garlic cloves, coarsely chopped

1 jalapeño, coarsely chopped

3/4 cup coarsely chopped flat-leaf parsley

2 bay leaves

3 medium Idaho potatoes, peeled and diced

1 quart Beef Stock (page 230)

Salt and freshly ground black pepper

Score the beef with 1/2-inch-wide incisions all over the top and bottom. In a food processor, combine the onion, orange juice, 4 tablespoons of the oil, garlic, jalapeño, 1/2 cup of the parsley, and the bay leaves and purée until smooth. Rub the marinade on both sides of the roast, making sure it gets into the incisions. Put the meat in a roasting pan, cover, and stick it in the refrigerator to marinate for at least 3 hours or overnight.

Preheat the oven to 400°F.

Remove the meat from the marinade and pat dry with paper towels. In a large Dutch oven or other ovenproof pot, heat the remaining 2 tablespoons of oil over a medium flame. When the oil begins to smoke, add the meat. Brown on all sides until a nice amber color has been achieved; this should take about 20 minutes. Add the potatoes and stock and give it a stir. Cover and roast in the oven for 1 1/2 hours. Remove the meat to a cutting board and let it cool down a bit. Using two forks, shred the beef and return it to the pot. Season with salt and pepper to taste and finish with the remaining 1/4 cup of chopped parsley before serving.

MONDONGO

The common trio of plantains, *calabaza*, and *malanga* make another appearance in this popular Caribbean stew. This dish originated in Puerto Rico and the Dominican Republic and is popular in the Washington Heights section of New York City, known as Little Santo Domingo.

SERVES 6

2 pounds honeycomb tripe, cut into 1-inch pieces (see Note)

1 cup freshly squeezed lemon juice (from about 10 lemons)

2 quarts plus 1 cup Chicken Broth (page 227)

4 tablespoons extra virgin olive oil

1 medium white onion, coarsely chopped

3 garlic cloves, minced

1 red bell pepper, cored and coarsely chopped

1 green bell pepper, cored and coarsely chopped

1 15-ounce can tomato purée

1/2 pound ham, cut into 1/2-inch cubes

1/4 pound *malanga* or taro root, peeled and cut into 1/2-inch chunks (see Note)

1/2 pound *calabaza*, peeled, cleaned, and cut into 1/2-inch chunks (see Note, page 43)

2 green plantains, peeled and cut into 1/2-inch slices (see Note)

Salt and freshly ground black pepper

2 tablespoons chopped cilantro

Put the tripe in a large bowl and add the lemon juice. Fill the bowl with water and let the tripe soak for 30 minutes. Remove from the lemon water, rinse, and put it in a large pot. Add the 2 quarts of broth and cook, covered, over medium-low heat for 2 hours, stirring occasionally.

Meanwhile, make a *sofrito:* Coat a large skillet with 2 tablespoons of the oil and place over medium heat. When the oil begins to smoke, add the onion, garlic, and peppers. Cook, stirring for 10 minutes, until the vegetables have softened. Stir in the tomato purée and cook for 15 minutes, then remove from the heat. When the mixture has cooled slightly, transfer to a food processor and purée until smooth.

In another large pot, heat the remaining 2 tablespoons of oil over a medium flame. When it is good and hot, add the ham and cook until it's crispy, about 10 minutes. Add the puréed pepper mixture and the tripe along with its broth. Bring up to a simmer. Add the *malanga, calabaza,* and plantains, and cook for 20 minutes, until the vegetables are tender. Add enough of the remaining cup of chicken broth to make the mixture soupy. Season with salt and pepper to taste, add the chopped cilantro, and serve.

TRIPE

The lining of the cow's stomach. This variety of meat is tough and requires long, slow cooking. Honeycomb tripe is from the second stomach chamber and is the most mildly flavored. Soaking the tripe in lemon breaks down the tough fibers, making the meat tender.

MALANGA ROOT

A yellowish-brown tuber often confused with taro because they look so similar. It's shaped like a sweet potato banded with circular shaggy ridges and has a nutty potato flavor with a high starch content. If *malanga* root is not available, substitute sweet potato.

TARO ROOT

Also called dasheen. It looks similar to its cousin *malanga,* with its brown fibrous skin and grayish flesh, but the shape is rounder. Often in Caribbean cooking, taro is served as the main starch, not as a vegetable. If taro root is not available, substitute sweet potato.

GREEN PLANTAIN

The large, firm variety of its cousin the banana. Commonly called the "cooking banana," this fruit is used mainly like a vegetable because it is quite starchy and has an almost squashlike flavor. Unripe plantains are green and hard. As they ripen, the skin starts to spot and changes from green to yellow, then eventually to black, while the flesh gets softer and sweeter. Green plantains and yellow-black sweet plantains are not to be used interchangeably, but *all* types of plantains must be cooked before eating.

To peel green plantains, score them lengthwise and submerge under boiling water for 20 minutes, or until the skin turns black. Drain and allow to cool slightly. Carefully run your thumb up the slits and the skin should peel away easily.

FRICASÉ DE POLLO

{chicken fricassée}

Fricassée is a classic French cooking method, and it is also a Cuban and Puerto Rican favorite. This homey stew is basically chicken in a pot, and it is found on many Cuban menus as a weekly special.

SERVES 4

- 1 whole frying chicken (about 3½ pounds), cut into 8 serving pieces
- 1 tablespoon salt
- 1½ teaspoons freshly ground black pepper
- ¼ cup extra-virgin olive oil
- 1 medium white onion, coarsely chopped
- 2 garlic cloves
- 1 red bell pepper, cored and coarsely chopped
- 1 green bell pepper, cored and coarsely chopped
- 1 *cubanella* or green bell pepper, cored and coarsely chopped
- 1 tablespoon ground cumin
- 1 tablespoon ground coriander
- 1 tablespoon cayenne
- ¼ pound *malanga* or taro root, peeled and cut into ½-inch chunks (see Note, page 55)
- ½ pound *calabaza*, peeled, cleaned, and cut into ½-inch chunks (see Note, page 43)
- 1 green plantain, peeled and cut into ½-inch slices (see Note, page 55)
- 1 quart Chicken Broth (page 227)
- ¼ cup chopped cilantro

Rinse the chicken pieces and pat them dry; season with the salt and pepper. Coat a large Dutch oven or other ovenproof pot with the oil and place over medium-high heat. When the oil just begins to smoke, add the chicken pieces, skin-side down; you may have to work in batches. Brown the chicken for 6 minutes on each side, then remove to a platter.

Preheat the oven to 375°F.

Return the pot to the stove over medium heat and add the onion, garlic, and peppers to the pan drippings. Cook, stirring, for 10 minutes, until the vegetables have softened; don't let them brown. Stir in the cumin, coriander, and cayenne, and cook for another 5 minutes. Transfer the mixture to a blender and purée until smooth (if necessary, add a little water to help get it going).

Return the browned chicken to the pot, along with the *malanga, calabaza,* and plantain. Pour in the chicken broth and the puréed pepper mixture. Cover and roast in the oven until the chicken is falling off the bone and the vegetables are tender, about 45 minutes to 1 hour. Season with salt and pepper to taste, shower with chopped cilantro, and serve.

THE MANY BARRIOS OF NEW YORK CITY

On the east side of Manhattan from about 96th Street to 125th Street, from Fifth Avenue to the East River, lies the neighborhood called Spanish Harlem, or El Barrio—the most well-known Latin-American area in the city. But it's far from the only Latin neighborhood in New York: there's Washington Heights in northern Manhattan, now known as Little Santo Domingo because of the growing number of transports from the Dominican Republic; Sunset Park, a primarily Mexican neighborhood in Brooklyn; and the Bronx, which has an immense Puerto Rican population. There's also the long stretch of Roosevelt Avenue in Queens, encompassing the neighborhoods of Jackson Heights and Corona, which is pan-Latin but with a pronounced Central and South American contingent (especially from Colombia, Ecuador, and Argentina); Union City, New Jersey, just across the Hudson River, with the second-largest (next to Miami) Cuban population in the United States; and the Lower East Side, where I have my restaurant, Paladar. Latin-Americans have been populating New York City in larger quantities than any other immigrants, and the barrio continues to thrive.

FEIJOADA COMPLETA

Feijoada is a bean potpourri-type dish that is without a doubt Brazil's culinary claim to fame. It is in fact so popular throughout Brazil that most restaurants, from the humblest inner-city luncheonettes to the sophisticated hotels lining Rio's shores, designate specific days on which this savory black-bean dish is served as the special. *Feijoada* is generally eaten as the main meal of the day, at lunchtime, because it is so filling. With several cuts of beef and pork, everyone around the table should get a little piece of everything. In an authentic *feijoada*, every part of the pig is thrown into the pan. Nothing goes to waste! To the dismay of the traditionalists, I have omitted pig's snout (and the like) to make the dish more mainstream and also to cut down on fat.

SERVES 10

2 pig's feet (about 2 pounds), halved (see Note, page 45)

1 smoked beef tongue (about 1½ pounds; see Note, page 51), or 2 smoked pork chops (about 1½ pounds), cut into 1-inch pieces

1 pound beef stew meat, top round or chuck, cut into 2-inch cubes

3 bay leaves

1 pound dried black turtle beans, picked through and rinsed

½ pound *carne seca* or *tasajo*, soaked and cut into 1-inch pieces (see Note)

1 pound *linguiça* or Spanish chorizo sausage (about 4 links), cut into 1-inch pieces (see Note, page 19)

1 tablespoon vegetable oil

½ pound bacon, diced

2 medium white onions, diced

4 garlic cloves, minced

1 serrano pepper, minced

2 oranges, peeled and cut in segments, for garnish
Cooked white rice, for serving

Put the pig's feet, tongue, beef cubes, and bay leaves in a large stockpot and cover with 3½ quarts of water. Simmer over medium heat, uncovered, for 1 hour, skimming any fat or foam that rises to the surface. Add the beans, *carne seca*, chorizo, and water if necessary to keep the ingredients covered. Cover and simmer for 1½ hours, until the beans are tender, skimming periodically.

Heat a skillet over a medium flame and coat with the oil. Add the bacon and fry for 5 minutes, until crispy. Add the onions, garlic, and serrano and cook, stirring, for 10 minutes, until the onion is soft. Add this mixture to the pot and give it a stir.

Remove the tongue, slice it, and then return it to the pot. Remove 2 cups of beans and liquid to a mixing bowl, crush with a potato masher, return to the pot, and stir to combine. Serve *feijoada* in large wide bowls, garnished with orange segments and accompanied by white rice.

CARNE SECA

Brazilian salted and cured beef, also called *machaca*. It is hard and dried and must be soaked overnight to soften and extract some of the salt; first scrape off the wax layer that covers it. If not available, substitute beef jerky.

SOUTH AMERICAN FOOD

The breadth of South America's many national cuisines is remarkably wide. There's Argentina's influences from Italy and other European countries; Brazil's Afro-Caribbean flavor; the Japanese inflections in Peru. And there's the importance of the pre-Hispanic foods—both potatoes and tomatoes were first cultivated here in the New World. But because the South American population in the United States isn't as large or well established as those in Mexico, Central America, and the Caribbean, South American food isn't as familiar to Americans, including me. So the recipes I've presented here—a handful from each of a few countries—are for dishes that have a true place in the barrios.

ESTOFADO DE **RABO** Y **POZOLE**

{braised oxtail and hominy stew}

Oxtail is a huge staple in Cuban cooking, and its presence on a menu in Miami is almost a given. I thought it would be great to combine some Mexican touches in this Cuban dish by adding *pozole* and *ancho* chiles. The oxtail meat can also be shredded and served in empanadas or over rice and beans. Short ribs, pork, or lamb shanks can be substituted for the oxtail.

SERVES 8 TO 10

6 *ancho* chiles, stemmed and seeded (see Note, page 49)
1 cup all-purpose flour
1 teaspoon ground cumin
1 teaspoon ground coriander
1 teaspoon cayenne
1 teaspoon garlic powder
2 pounds oxtails, trimmed of excess fat and cut into 2-inch pieces
3 tablespoons extra-virgin olive oil
1 medium white onion, coarsely chopped
2 carrots, coarsely chopped
4 celery stalks, coarsely chopped
2 garlic cloves, smashed
2 cups dry red wine, such as Merlot
3 quarts Beef Stock (page 230)
1 15-ounce can chopped tomatoes
1 15-ounce can hominy (see Note)
  Salt and freshly ground black pepper
2 tablespoons chopped flat-leaf parsley, for garnish

Bring 2 cups of water to a boil. In a dry cast-iron skillet, toast the chiles over medium-low heat for 5 minutes, until fragrant; turn them and shake the pan so they don't scorch. Put the toasted chiles in a bowl, cover with the boiling water, and let soak until softened and reconstituted, about 20 minutes. Put the chiles, along with 1 cup of the soaking water, in a blender and purée until completely smooth; you may have to do this in batches. Set aside.

Preheat the oven to 350°F.

In a large shallow platter, mix the flour with the cumin, coriander, cayenne, and garlic powder. Dredge the oxtails in the seasoned flour to coat, shaking off the excess. Heat the oil in a large Dutch oven or other ovenproof pot over medium-high flame. When the oil begins to smoke, add the oxtails in batches, making sure not to crowd the pan. Cook on each side for 5 minutes, until golden brown, then remove to a platter. Add the onion, carrots, celery, and garlic to the pan drippings, lower the heat to medium, and cook for 10 minutes, until the vegetables are caramelized.

Pour in the wine, stock, tomatoes, hominy, and chile purée. Bring the liquid up to a simmer, then return the oxtails to the pot. Cover and roast in the oven for 45 minutes to 1 hour, until the meat is falling off the bone. Season with salt and pepper to taste, shower with some chopped parsley, and serve.

HOMINY OR POZOLE

Dried white corn kernels from which the hull and germ have been removed by soaking the corn in slaked lime, called cal. Hominy is starchy and not as sweet as regular corn; it is sold canned and ready to eat, or dried (which must be boiled before using and is more difficult to obtain).

MIAMI'S CALLE OCHO FESTIVAL

El Festival de la Calle Ocho, as it is commonly known to many, celebrates the heritage and living traditions of the Cuban community in Florida. Calle Ocho, Spanish for "Eighth Street," is the most popular street in Little Havana, Miami's center of Cuban culture. Started in 1978, this street party is the largest Hispanic festival held in the United States and has become a cultural celebration of everything Latino. It's a partygoer's dream, full of music, dancing, and of course food. With more than a million people attending each year, it is a major tourist attraction, providing an opportunity to savor the flavor of Carnival Miami.

PIPIÁN DE CHULETAS DE PUERCO

{pork chops in green chile sauce}

There are as many variations of moles as there are curries in India, each with its own distinctive color, flavor, and aroma. *Mole verde* is most commonly prepared in the states of Puebla, Tlaxcala, and Oaxaca, where it is one of *los siete moles*—the seven famous moles. The thick green sauce is made from pumpkin seeds, *poblanos,* tomatillos, fresh herbs, and sometimes even lettuce leaves for an added vibrant green color. This mole is very similar to the pre-Hispanic sauce called *pipián,* whose main ingredient is toasted and ground *pepitas.* I often find the terms mole and *pipián* interchanged. Deep green mole has a bold flavor that matches well with lean meats such as turkey, chicken, and lean cuts of pork.

SERVES 4

1	medium white onion, peeled and halved
4	garlic cloves, peeled
20	small tomatillos, husked and rinsed
1	jalapeño
3/4	cup extra-virgin olive oil
1	*poblano* pepper (see Note, page 85)
1	cup *pepitas* (raw hulled green pumpkin seeds), roasted and salted (see page 33)
2	cups coarsely chopped cilantro
2	tablespoons dried epazote (see Note, page 85)
2	quarts Chicken Broth (page 227)
2	tablespoons lard (page 224)
1 1/2	tablespoons salt
4	bone-in pork chops, about 1/2 inch thick
1 1/2	teaspoons freshly ground black pepper

Put a dry skillet over a medium-high flame and let it get nice and hot, a good 2 minutes. Rub the onion, garlic, tomatillos, and jalapeño with 1/2 cup of the oil. Lay the vegetables in the hot pan and roast, turning occasionally, until soft and well charred on all sides, about 10 minutes. Put the vegetables in a bowl to let them cool a bit. Peel the skin from the jalapeño and remove the stem. Transfer to a blender and purée in batches until completely smooth. Put the batches of purée in a large container as you work.

Rub the *poblano* with 2 tablespoons of the oil and roast on a very hot grill, over a gas flame, or under a broiler until the skin is blistered and blackened on all sides. Put the pepper in a bowl, cover with plastic wrap, and let sweat for about 10 minutes to loosen the skin. Peel and rub off the charred skin, pull out the core, and remove the seeds. Put the *poblano,* along with any collected juices, in the blender and purée until smooth; add to the roasted-vegetable mixture.

Purée the *pepitas,* cilantro, epazote, and 2 cups of the broth together in the blender until thick and smooth; mix into the pepper purée.

Melt the lard in a large Dutch oven or deep skillet over medium heat and pour in the purée; be careful because it may spatter a little. Cook and stir for 5 minutes, until the mole deepens in color. Add the remaining 6 cups of broth and 1 tablespoon of salt and simmer for 10 minutes to thicken, stirring occasionally.

Season the pork chops with the pepper and the remaining 1½ teaspoons of salt. Place a large skillet over medium-high heat and coat with the remaining 2 tablespoons of oil. When the oil begins to smoke, panfry the pork chops for 2 minutes on each side to form a crust. Transfer the chops to the mole and simmer for 15 minutes to cook through.

SOPA DE **MARISCOS**

{seafood stew}

Main-dish seafood stews are featured in many restaurants along the Gulf of Mexico, where locals are able to capture the flavor of the freshest catch of the day. In inner-city neighborhoods, where fish is not as bountiful and therefore is more expensive, seafood stew is typically served as a summer weekend meal. Like all fisherman's stews, practically any assortment of ocean life works here, as long as the product is fresh and of good quality. As a guide, I suggest pairing briny shellfish with buttery fish fillets; I have charmed many taste buds at Paladar by folding calamari into the mix. This soup has the licorice flavor characteristic of classic Provençal bouillabaisse due to the saffron — don't leave it out; it's an integral part of the dish. Serve with Yellow Rice (page 158) or a big slice of crusty bread.

SERVES 4

2 tablespoons extra-virgin olive oil

½ medium white onion, sliced

2 garlic cloves, smashed

2 dozen littleneck clams, washed and scrubbed

3 pounds mussels, washed, scrubbed, and debearded

1 cup dry white wine such as sauvignon blanc

1 teaspoon saffron threads

2 ears fresh corn, shucked

1 canned *chipotle* in adobo (see Note, page 71), minced

2 quarts Shrimp Stock (page 229)

1 Idaho potato, peeled and diced

8 medium shrimp (about ½ pound), peeled and deveined with tails on

1 pound fish fillets, such as grouper, cod, or sea bass, cut into ½-inch chunks

6 cherry tomatoes, halved

4 scallions, white and green parts, chopped

Juice of 1 lime

¼ cup chopped cilantro

Salt and freshly ground black pepper

Coat a large stockpot with the oil and heat over a medium flame. Add the onion and garlic, and stir for 2 minutes to soften. Put the clams and mussels in the pot and turn them over with a wooden spoon to coat in the onion mixture. Add the wine and saffron, cover, and cook for 5 minutes to steam the clams and mussels open. Add the corn, *chipotle*, and stock; bring up to a simmer. Add the potato and simmer, uncovered, for 5 minutes. Add the shrimp, fish fillets, tomatoes, and scallions, stir everything together, and cook for 5 minutes, until the shrimp are firm and the fish opaque. Finish with the lime and cilantro, and season with salt and pepper to taste.

PARA LLEVAR

Many places in the barrio offer things to go, or *para llevar*, especially those that require a lot of ingredients or a long time to cook: a slow-roasted *barba-coa*, a succulent roast pork. You buy these by the pound, along with some tor-tillas, and serve them at home with homemade rice and beans. These to-go joints usually have one special per day—Tuesdays it's *chuleta*, Wednesdays it's *pernil*—that you can count on. Since you can't get a given dish except on the appropriate day, you love its weekly appearance all the more. Just try being in the mood for *lechón asado* on the wrong day of the week. Buying food *para llevar* is as easy as eating out, but you also get the benefits of stay-ing in, with your family.

{the street stand: tacos, tamales, and other snacks}

TA█OS DE CAZÓN
{shark tacos}

TA█OS DE CÉCINA
{pounded pork tacos}

U█HEPOS
{fresh corn tamales}

TAMALES DE MOLE AMARILLO
{tamales with yellow mole sauce}

TA█OS DE CARNE ASADA
{roasted beef tacos}

PASTELES PUERTORRIQUEÑOS
{puerto rican tamales}

TAMALES DE RAJAS
{tamales with roasted poblano strips}

T█RTA DE HUEVO Y CHORIZO
{egg and chorizo sandwich}

G█RDITAS
{corn flour patties}

S█PES
{corn tarts}

PUPUSAS
{stuffed corn turnovers}

TORTA MILANESA
{breaded steak sandwich}

CROQUETAS DE JAMÓN
{ham croquettes}

PAN CON LECHÓN
{roast pork sandwiches}

CROQUETAS DE PESCADO
{fish croquettes}

ANTICUCHOS DE POLLO
{grilled chicken skewers}

SANDWICH CUBANO
{cuban sandwich}

CHICHARRÓNES
{fried pork rinds}

ALCAPURRÍAS
{green plantain dumplings}

I THINK MUCH OF THE best food in the world is street food—

the portable snacks you buy from carts on the sidewalk, or from little shops with just a couple of specialties. Every culture has its own street food, from Chinese buns to Italian *panini.* Mexican-Americans have a remarkable variety of them—*tortas* and tamales, *gorditas* and *sopes,* and of course tacos, the namesake snack.

The *taquería* is found in Latin neighborhoods throughout the Western hemisphere. There's usually an open kitchen, so you can see what's going on, and a menu with plenty of choices. Nearly every dish is some type of starch, stuffed with meat or chicken, and usually sauced.

Some taquerías may specialize in great *tortas,* some in perfectly moist tamales, but most are known for their tacos. You get a choice of about a half dozen fillings—marinated pork, roasted beef, sauced chicken. The preparation is very strict: two tortillas—small, white-corn ones (not big ones, not yellow-corn, not flour)—are moistened with lard and heated on a lard-brushed griddle; the tortillas are doubled up and wrapped around the filling of your choice, topped with chopped white onion, cilantro, and a puréed red or green salsa if the filling is a roasted meat; and served with lime wedges on the side. No cheese, no sour cream, no rice, no beans. On the counter, there are little bowls of self-serve garnishes: marinated red onions, pickled jalapeños, marinated chile de árbol, and salsas (a green one made with tomatillo and jalapeño, a red one based on puréed roasted tomatoes). The key to the taco's success is the doubling up of tortillas—something that home cooks often forget. Just one small corn tortilla isn't sturdy enough to hold enough filling for a satisfying taco—not only will the taco fall apart after your first bite, but the filling won't be properly balanced with enough of the *masa.* Use two.

You get two or three tacos in an order. You can eat them standing up at a counter, sitting down at a table, or walking down the street. If you're hungry and have a big mouth, you can swallow a taco in just a couple of bites—the first taco I eat usually disappears in about fifteen seconds. You get a little protein, a little starch, a little vegetable, and a lot of flavor in every bite, in perfect proportions.

TACOS DE **CAZÓN**

Fish tacos are eaten primarily in Baja California and the area that surrounds the Pacific, but their immense popularity has led to their appearance in *taquerías* all over the United States. Fish tacos are usually made with a firm, meaty fish, such as shark or mahimahi, which is battered and fried, then rolled in a tortilla. Personally, I think this cooking method makes the taco greasy and soggy, and masks the true essence of the fish. This lighter version of marinating the fish and then grilling brings out more flavors. If shark or mahimahi are not available, use whatever looks and smells the freshest locally. You will need 12 wooden skewers to make this recipe; soak the sticks in water for 20 minutes to prevent them from burning.

SERVES 4 (2 PER PERSON)

2 pounds shark, mako, or thresher, cut into 1/4-inch cubes (about 60 pieces)

1 tablespoon salt

1 tablespoon freshly ground black pepper

2 canned *chipotles* plus 2 teaspoons adobo (see Note)

3 garlic cloves

Finely grated zest of 1 lime

1 cup chopped cilantro

1/2 cup extra-virgin olive oil, plus more for coating the pan

16 corn tortillas

1 medium white onion, chopped

2 limes, cut into wedges, for serving

Thread 5 or 6 chunks of fish onto each soaked skewer (see headnote). Put the shark on a platter and season with the salt and pepper.

In a blender, combine the *chipotles* and adobo, garlic, lime zest, 1/2 cup of cilantro, and the oil, and purée until smooth. Pour the *chipotle* mixture over the fish, cover, and refrigerate for at least 1 hour or up to 8 hours.

Preheat an outdoor grill or a ridged grill pan over a medium-high flame. Brush the grates with a little oil to prevent the fish from sticking. Remove the shark from the marinade and grill for 3 minutes on each side. Push the shark cubes off the skewers.

Heat a large dry skillet over a medium flame. Warm the tortillas for 30 seconds on each side, until toasty and pliable.

To make the tacos, stack 2 warm tortillas, lay 5 or 6 chunks of shark down the center, sprinkle with some chopped onion and the remaining cilantro, and garnish with lime wedges. Repeat with the remaining tortillas.

CHIPOTLE CHILES

Dried and smoked jalapeños. They have a full, almost tobaccolike flavor and a subtle heat that creeps up on you. They are most commonly found canned in rusty-red adobo, which is a slightly sweet sauce made from tomatoes and vinegar. You can also purchase them dried and reconstitute them in boiling water until soft and pliable before using.

TACOS DE **CÉCINA**

{pounded pork tacos}

Mexican tacos are usually soft-shelled, unlike the U-shaped crisp-fried tortillas served in many American restaurants and fast-food joints. Some Mexican butcher shops sell already marinated pork tenderloin—you can spot it by the meat's rich red color imparted from the chile paste; this marinated tenderloin is also used in tortas (page 87). Pork and lime is one of those great flavor combinations that I am addicted to, and because the meat is pounded, it absorbs the marinade all the way through and cooks really quickly. Bear in mind that you'll need to marinate the pork overnight, so plan accordingly.

SERVES 4 (2 PER PERSON)

- 2 *guajillo* chiles, stemmed and seeded (see Note, page 121)
- 2 pork tenderloins (about 1 pound each)
- 1 tablespoon white vinegar
- 1 teaspoon dried Mexican oregano (see Note)
- 2 tablespoons extra-virgin olive oil, plus more for coating the pan
- 1 teaspoon salt
- ½ teaspoon freshly ground black pepper
- 16 corn tortillas
- 1 medium white onion, chopped
- ½ cup chopped cilantro
- 2 limes, cut in wedges, for serving

Bring 1 cup of water to a boil. In a dry cast-iron skillet, toast the chiles over medium-low heat for 2 minutes, until fragrant; turn them and shake the pan so they don't scorch. Put the toasted chiles in a bowl, cover with the boiling water, and let them soak until softened and reconstituted, about 15 minutes.

Using a sharp knife, make a deep slit down the length of the tenderloins and open them up so they lay flat. With the smooth side of a mallet, pound the pork between two pieces of plastic to a ¼-inch thickness. Transfer to a platter.

In a blender, combine the toasted chiles, vinegar, oregano, 2 tablespoons of oil, salt, and pepper, and purée to form a paste. Rub the paste on both sides of the pork. Cover with plastic wrap and refrigerate overnight.

Preheat an outdoor grill or a ridged grill pan over a medium-high flame. Brush the grates with a little oil to prevent the meat from sticking. Scrape off the excess chile paste from the pork and grill it for 2 minutes per side. Remove to a cutting board and let it rest for 2 minutes to allow the juices to settle, then slice it into ¼-inch pieces.

Heat a large dry skillet over a medium flame. Warm the tortillas for 30 seconds on each side, until toasty and pliable.

To make the tacos, stack 2 warm tortillas, lay about 4 ounces of pork down the center, sprinkle with some chopped onion and cilantro, and garnish with lime wedges. Repeat with the remaining tortillas.

MEXICAN OREGANO

A dried herb with a strong, aromatic flavor; also referred to as wild marjoram. It was a staple in my childhood home in El Paso. When my mother was growing up on a northern Mexican ranch, the cattle used to graze on fresh wild-growing oregano, so as a result, the meat itself had a subtle oregano flavor.

MEXICAN STREET FOOD IN THE MISSION

There's nothing quite like walking around the Mission on a nice weekend day, taking in the sights of this vibrant neighborhood: the street murals of Aztec warriors, civil-rights activists, and neighborhood heroes; the mothers toting their *mercado* bags, bargaining for plantains, cheeses, and chilies; the kids surrounding the carts of crushed ices. At Valencia and Twenty-fourth, a woman sells some of the great staples of Mexican street food: cups of jicama, cucumber, and mango spears, as well as sliced mango in plastic bags, which she tosses to taste with fresh lime juice, chili powder, and salt—water-filled foods that are perfect on a hot day. The bags of mango are a buck apiece, and she dresses each serving without asking you how you want it; she senses by instinct the right proportions for each customer of the four elemental flavors—hot, sour, salty, and sweet, here represented by just one simple ingredient apiece.

UCHEPOS

No *masa* or dried cornhusks are used for this completely fresh tamale, which is from the Michoacán region of Mexico. And there's no lard in this recipe, but plenty of butter! *Uchepos* are often prepared during the summer months, when corn is at its peak in flavor and sweetness. The Aztecs, known as "men of corn," planned their yearly calendar around corn harvesting.

SERVES 6 (2 PER PERSON)

- 12 ears fresh corn, unhusked
- 1 cup (2 sticks) unsalted butter, at room temperature
- 2 tablespoons sugar
- 1 tablespoon salt
- 1 cup crumbled *queso fresco* (see Note)

Carefully peel the husks off the corn. Select 12 of the largest outer husks and cover them with a damp cloth. Cut the kernels off the cob with a sharp knife, put the kernels in a food processor, and purée until smooth.

In the bowl of an electric mixer, beat the soft butter until it starts to form ribbons. Beat in the sugar and salt. Pour in the puréed corn and continue to mix until incorporated, about 2 minutes.

Spread about 3 tablespoons of the corn mixture on the inside of the reserved cornhusks. Fold the sides in first, then fold the top and bottom into the center. Tie securely with kitchen twine to hold the husk closed.

Bring a large pot filled with 2 inches of water to a simmer. Stand the *uchepos* up in a steamer or colander and put it into the pot, but don't let the water touch the bottoms of the *uchepos*. Cover tightly with a lid and steam for 20 minutes over medium-low heat, or until firm. Uncover and let cool in the steamer for 10 minutes. To serve, unfold the husk and top with a little crumbled *queso fresco*.

QUESO FRESCO AND QUESO BLANCO

Queso fresco is a salty and mildly acidic fresh cheese used widely in Latin America. Introduced to Mexico from Burgos, Spain, this spongy, tangy white cheese is made from cow's milk. It's great to crumble on top of dishes or in fillings because when heated it becomes soft and creamy, not melted and gooey. A very mild feta is an acceptable substitute. Queso blanco, on the other hand, is very similar to mozzarella—a great melting cheese. When you see simply the word *queso*, like on a *torta*, chances are it's referring to *blanco*.

TAMALES DE **MOLE AMARILLO**

{tamales with yellow mole sauce}

This recipe is a hybrid of two different influences. The tamales themselves have roots in the conventional tamales with mole that I grew up enjoying at Mexican family restaurants in Texas. But I've adapted this Oaxacan mole served on the Day of the Dead and paired it with the tamales from my childhood. The mild *guajillo* chile is used in this mole predominantly for its vibrant yellow-orange color, earning it the title "Amarillo."

SERVES 6 (2 PER PERSON)

1	8-ounce package dried cornhusks
2	cups *masa harina* (see Note)
2	teaspoons salt
1½	cups warm Chicken Broth (page 227)
¼	cup lard (page 224)
1½	cups *Mole Amarillo* (recipe follows)
1½	cups shredded cooked chicken (page 226)
2	large fresh or 5 dried *hoja santa* leaves, coarsely chopped (see Note)

Separate the cornhusks from one another and discard the silk—be careful since the papery husks break easily when they are dry. Select 12 of the biggest and best-looking husks from the bunch and soak them in a large bowl or sink filled with warm water for 30 minutes to soften.

To make the dough, in a deep bowl, combine the *masa* and salt. Pour the warm broth into the *masa* a little at a time, working it in with your fingers. In a small bowl, beat the lard with a hand mixer until fluffy, add it to the *masa*, and mix until the dough has a spongy texture.

To make the tamales, drain the cornhusks and pat dry with paper towels. Lay a husk flat on a plate or in your hand with the smooth side up and the narrow end facing you. Spread a thin, even layer of *masa* over the surface of the husk with a spoon that has been dipped in water. Down the center of the *masa*, add a spoonful each of the mole sauce, the shredded chicken, and the chopped *santa* leaves. Fold the narrow end up to the center, then fold both sides together to enclose the filling, and pinch the wide top closed; the sticky *masa* will form a seal. Repeat with the remaining husks.

Bring a large pot filled with 2 inches of water to a simmer. Stand the tamales up in a steamer or colander and put it into the pot, but don't let the water touch the bottoms of the tamales. Lay a damp cloth over the tamales, cover tightly with a lid, and steam for 30 minutes over medium-low heat; keep the water at a low simmer. The tamales are done when the inside pulls away from the husk; they should be soft but still firm and not mushy. Turn off the heat, remove the cover and damp towel, and let cool in the steamer for 10 minutes. To serve, unfold the husk and spoon a tablespoon of mole sauce on top of each.

MASA HARINA

Dehydrated, powdered *masa*, often referred to as instant corn *masa*. (Broadly, *masa* means "dough" in Spanish, but specifically, the word is often synonymous with corn dough.) Maseca is a popular brand and can be found in most grocery stores. The flour is made from cooked ground hominy and looks like white cornmeal.

HOJA SANTA LEAVES

Sometimes called *acuyo* or *hanepa* in some regions of Mexico; also known as Mexican pepper leaf. This aromatic herb, which means "sacred leaf" literally translated, is much used in the cuisines of tropical Mexico. Unfortunately, it's not widely available outside the region of origin (southern Mexico, Guatemala, Panama, and northern Colombia). The flavor is loosely reminiscent of anise, black pepper, and nutmeg; when fresh, the leaves look like big lily pads. Fresh or dried tarragon can be substituted (use 2 tablespoons fresh or 1 tablespoon dried).

mole amarillo

{yellow mole}

If making mole intimidates you, relax in knowing that it gets better with age, so you can prepare it a couple of days ahead. Contrary to popular belief, not all moles contain chocolate (all do, however, contain chiles); in Spanish, *mole* means "to grind." *Masa harina* thickens the sauce, much like all-purpose flour is used as a thickening agent in classic French sauces. But what is very un-French is frying the mole in hot lard, a crucial step that takes away the raw taste of the chiles and brings together the complex flavors of all the ingredients.

MAKES 2 QUARTS

3 *guajillo* chiles, stemmed and seeded (see Note, page 121)
1 *ancho* chile, stemmed and seeded (see Note, page 49)
1 medium white onion, peeled and halved
4 garlic cloves, peeled
4 medium tomatillos, husked and rinsed
1 green or red tomato, halved
¼ cup extra-virgin olive oil
1 teaspoon whole black peppercorns
5 whole cloves
2 tablespoons lard (page 224)
2 tablespoons *masa harina* (see Note, page 77)

Bring 2 cups of water to a boil. In a dry cast-iron skillet, toast the *guajillo* and *ancho* chiles over medium-low heat for 2 minutes, until fragrant; turn them and shake the pan so they don't scorch. Put the toasted chiles in a bowl, cover with the boiling water, and let soak until softened and reconstituted, about 20 minutes.

Return the skillet to medium-high heat and let it get nice and hot, a good 2 minutes. Rub the onion, garlic, tomatillos, and tomato with the oil. Lay the vegetables in the hot pan and roast, turning occasionally, until soft and well charred on all sides, about 10 minutes. Put the vegetables in a bowl to let them cool a bit.

Meanwhile, grind the peppercorns and cloves in a clean coffee grinder or spice mill.

Put all the components together in a blender—the chiles along with their soaking water, the charred vegetables, and the ground spices. Purée in batches until completely smooth.

Melt the lard in a skillet over medium heat and pour in the purée; be careful because it may spatter a little. Cook and stir for 5 minutes, until the mole deepens in color.

In a small bowl, mix the *masa harina* with ¼ cup of warm water until smooth and lump-free. Whisk the slurry into the sauce and continue to simmer for 5 more minutes, until the sauce is slightly thickened and able to coat the back of a spoon.

TACOS DE **CARNE ASADA**

{roasted beef tacos}

Tacos de carne asada are the most popular item ordered in a *taquería*. During the summer, when most American families gather outdoors for cookouts with hamburgers and hot dogs, Mexican-Americans include *carne asada* as their barbecue staple. Marinating the steak in the pickled jalapeño mixture is the key to the beef's intense flavor and tender texture. The vegetables impart a spicy sweetness, while the vinegar in the brine tenderizes the tough cut of meat. Don't marinate for more than 8 hours, though, or the fibers break down too much and the meat gets mushy.

SERVES 4 (2 PER PERSON)

- 2 pounds flank steak, trimmed of excess fat
- 1 cup canned pickled jalapeños, including the carrots and onions that come with it (see Note, page 139)
  Extra-virgin olive oil for coating the pan
- 1 tablespoon salt
- 1 tablespoon freshly ground black pepper
- 16 corn tortillas
- 1 medium white onion, chopped
- ½ cup chopped cilantro
- ¼ cup *Salsa de Árbol* (page 231)
- 2 limes, cut in wedges, for serving

Lay the flank steak on a flat surface and cover it with the jalapeño mixture, then roll the meat up like a pinwheel. Wrap tightly in plastic wrap and refrigerate for 1 hour or up to 8 hours, so the flavors can sink into the meat.

Preheat an outdoor grill or a ridged grill pan over a medium-high flame (you can also use a broiler). Brush the grates with a little oil to prevent the meat from sticking. Unroll the flank steak and scrape off the jalapeño mixture. Season the steak on both sides with the salt and pepper. Grill (or broil) for 7 to 10 minutes per side, turning once, until medium-rare. Remove to a cutting board and let rest for 5 minutes to allow the juices to settle, then slice across the grain into ¼-inch-thick pieces.

Heat a large dry skillet over a medium flame. Warm the tortillas for 30 seconds on each side, until toasty and pliable.

To make the tacos, stack 2 warm tortillas, lay about 4 ounces of beef down the center, and sprinkle with some onion and cilantro. Drizzle 1½ teaspoons of the *Salsa de Árbol* on top of each taco and garnish with lime wedges.

Californians will tell you that what New York lacks is a good *taquería*. They have a point—it's a lot easier to come by a solid taco on the Left Coast than the Right. But if they say it's impossible to find a good taco here, they haven't taken the Number 6 train uptown to Taco Mix, at 116th Street and First Avenue, as I recently did with a magazine writer who ended up penning "Looking for the Perfect Taco" for *Time Out New York*.

Like most Mexican places uptown, Taco Mix serves a mix of tacos, tamales, and tortas—the three T's of Mexican snacks. What makes Taco Mix outstanding is its rotating griddle with the luxurious bonus of lard in the middle, which helps moisten meats like pig's ear, *carne asada* (grilled beef), and *chile pastor* (marinated pork). Tacos are made with doubled-up corn tortillas, garnished from an adjoining counter laden with marinated onions with chile de árbol and a choice of puréed salsas made from tomatillos or red tomatoes, of varying heat.

For two dollars, you get three small tacos. In the winter, people line up at a quick-serve window outside, or huddle inside to wait for a table. In summer, the restaurant provides outdoor carts, so you can order and enjoy your superb taco without having to miss a moment of the energetic sights and sounds of the barrio. Looking for the perfect taco? You can buy it at Taco Mix, or try one of the recipes in this chapter.

PASTELES PUERTORRIQUEÑOS

{puerto rican tamales}

Traditional holiday recipes are, of course, the most time-consuming and labor intensive. But the outcome is well worth the trouble for special-occasion meals: A variety of *pasteles* are sold every year at the Puerto Rican Day parade in New York City. *Pasteles* are also made with *viandas*, which are root vegetables such as yautia, yuca, and *bonaito*. I had the pleasure of learning a version of these *pasteles* from one of the servers at my restaurant, Midgi Lamboy.

MAKES 1 DOZEN
SERVES 12 AS AN APPETIZER

FILLING

	Juice of 8 Seville oranges (about 1 cup; see Note)
2	garlic cloves, minced
1	tablespoon dried Mexican oregano (see Note, page 73)
1	tablespoon salt
1	teaspoon freshly ground black pepper
1	pound pork butt, cut into ½-inch cubes
1½	cups *achiote* oil (page 225)
1	medium white onion, diced
1	green bell pepper, cored and diced
2	ripe tomatoes, chopped
2	cups Chicken Broth (page 227)
½	cup coarsely chopped cilantro
1	15-ounce can garbanzo beans
12	pimiento-stuffed green olives
½	cup raisins
2	tablespoons capers, drained

DOUGH

2	pounds white plus 2 pounds yellow yautia, peeled and cut into 1-inch chunks (see Note, page 107)
7	green plantains, peeled and cut into 1-inch chunks (see Note, page 55)
1	cup warm whole milk
1	tablespoon salt
	1-pound package banana leaves (see Note, page 121)

To make the filling, in a medium bowl, mix together the orange juice, garlic, oregano, salt, and pepper. Place the pork in a shallow glass dish, pour the marinade over, cover, and refrigerate for 1 hour.

Preheat the oven to 350°F.

In a large Dutch oven or other ovenproof pot, heat ½ cup of the *achiote* oil over a medium flame. Drain the pork from the marinade and fry for about 10 minutes, turning with a tongs until evenly browned on all sides. Add the onion, pepper, and tomatoes, and cook for 8 minutes, until the vegetables soften. Add the broth, cilantro, garbanzos, olives, raisins, and capers. Cover, transfer to the oven, and cook for 45 minutes, until the meat is tender and the liquid is nearly evaporated.

To make the dough, purée both types of yautia with the plantains and milk in a food processor; it is best to do this in batches. The dough should be like a smooth paste. Transfer the mixture to a large bowl, add the salt and remaining 1 cup of *achiote* oil, and mix well, until the dough is an even yellow-orange color.

To form the pasteles, clean and cut the banana leaves into 10 × 6-inch rectangles. Cut a piece of wax paper slightly bigger and put a banana leaf on top. Spread 3 tablespoons of the root vegetable paste thinly on the leaf, leaving a ½-inch border all around the edges. Put 3 tablespoons of the pork filling down the center of the paste, and top with an additional tablespoon of the paste to cover. Fold the banana leaf in half lengthwise, using the wax paper for support. Fold the ends into the center so they barely touch, taking care that by folding you do not apply too much pressure and cause the filling to ooze out. The pasteles should look like little envelopes. Using kitchen string, tie the pasteles crisscross like a gift, so that both ends are sealed completely.

Bring a large pot of salted water to a boil. Add the pasteles, cover, and cook for 30 minutes, until firm when pressed. Once cooked, remove promptly from the water and let them rest for 10 minutes before unwrapping and serving.

SEVILLE ORANGES

Tart oranges grown in the Mediterranean that are also called sour and bitter oranges. They are relatively small and contain only about 2 tablespoons of potent juice per orange. Sour oranges are used daily in the Cuban and Caribbean kitchen because of their unique sweet, sour, and acidic flavor. They are also the orange of choice from which to make marmalade. If Seville oranges are not available, mix equal parts of fresh orange and lime juices.

TAMALES DE **RAJAS**

{tamales with roasted poblano strips}

Rajas means "strips" in Spanish, and generally refers to roasted *poblano* peppers cut into strips in the Mexican kitchen. The peppers are the star of this tamale because there is no meat in the filling. *Rajas* are eaten in many different ways, most often as an accompaniment to a grilled steak or as a side component to a dish.

MAKES 1 DOZEN

1 8-ounce package dried cornhusks
2 cups *masa harina* (see Note, page 77)
2 teaspoons salt, plus more to taste
1½ cups warm Chicken Broth (page 227)
¼ cup lard (page 224) or vegetable shortening
2 tablespoons canola oil, plus more for rubbing the peppers
4 *poblano* peppers (see Note)
1 medium white onion, thinly sliced
2 garlic cloves, slivered
1 tablespoon dried epazote (see Note)
1 cup heavy cream
1 cup grated Jack cheese
  Freshly ground black pepper

Separate the cornhusks and discard the silk—be careful since the papery husks break easily when they are dry. Select 12 of the biggest and best-looking husks from the bunch and soak them in a large bowl or sink filled with warm water for 30 minutes to soften.

In a deep bowl, combine the *masa* and salt. Pour the warm broth into the *masa* a little at a time, working it in with your fingers. In a small bowl, beat the lard with a hand mixer until fluffy, add it to the *masa,* and mix until the dough has a spongy texture. Cover and set aside.

Rub the *poblano* peppers with oil and roast on a very hot grill, over a gas flame, or under a broiler until the skin is blistered and blackened on all sides. Put the peppers in a bowl, cover with plastic wrap, and let sweat for about 10 minutes to loosen the skins. Peel and rub off the charred skin, pull out the cores, and remove the seeds. Cut the peppers into ¼-inch strips.

In a deep skillet or pot, heat 2 tablespoons of canola oil over medium flame. Add the onion, garlic, and epazote, and cook for 5 minutes, until soft. Add the pepper strips, and sauté for 2 minutes to combine. Stir in the cream and cook for 2 minutes, until steam rises from the pan. Remove the pan from the heat and fold in the cheese until melted, thick, and creamy; season with salt and pepper to taste.

To make the tamales, drain the cornhusks and pat dry with paper towels. Lay a husk flat on a plate or in your hand with the smooth side up and the narrow end facing you. Spread a thin, even layer of the *masa* mixture over the surface of the husk with a spoon that has been dipped in water. Add a spoonful of the *rajas* filling down the center of the *masa*. Fold the narrow end up to the center, then fold both sides together to enclose the filling and pinch the wide top closed; the sticky *masa* will form a seal. Repeat with the remaining husks.

Bring a large pot filled with 2 inches of water to a simmer. Stand the tamales up in a steamer or colander and put it into the pot, but don't let the water touch the bottoms of the tamales. Lay a damp cloth over the tamales, cover tightly with a lid, and steam for 30 minutes over medium-low heat; keep the water at a low simmer. The tamales are done when the inside pulls away from the husk; they should be soft but still firm and not mushy. Shut off the heat, remove the cover and damp towel, and let cool in the steamer for 10 minutes before serving.

POBLANO

Translates to "pepper from Puebla," the region in Mexico where it originates. This fresh blackish-green chile is one of the most popular in Mexican cooking. It is about the size of a green bell pepper but is more heart-shaped, with a flavor that's deeper than a bell pepper without being overly hot. In its dried state, poblanos are known as *ancho* chiles. Do not under any circumstances peel *poblanos* under running water, which would remove all of the great smoky-charred flavor.

EPAZOTE

Also known as Mexican tea, a native herb with jagged, unusual-shaped leaves. Pungent-tasting with a hint of lemon and anise, it may take a little getting used to. This herb is sometimes referred to as the "stink weed"—it grows rampant in the Mexican countryside and has a "distinctive" odor. It is commonly used in bean dishes because it reduces the amount of gas that beans can provoke. Epazote is sold in small packages in its dried form and in bunches when fresh; either way, you want to pull off the leaves and discard the stems. Before adding it to dishes, rub the leaves in your hands to release the herb's natural oils. There really is no substitute for epazote, but if hard pressed, use tarragon.

TORTA DE **HUEVO** Y **CHORIZO**

{egg and chorizo sandwich}

This hero sandwich is eaten at all times of the day, including breakfast. *Bolillo* is the name of the Mexican-style roll (it is diamond-shaped like a Portuguese roll), which is moistened with hot refried beans and creamy avocado. The dressings or accompaniments are pretty standard for all tortas: lettuce, pickled jalapeño, beans, avocado, and mayonnaise. The meat varies from one to the next, but pork is most common because it's always available in the Latin kitchen. Use the pounded pork from *Tacos de Cécina* (page 72) or the *pernil* or *lechón* (pages 118 and 119).

SERVES 4

- 2 tablespoons canola oil, plus more for brushing the rolls
- 1 pound Spanish chorizo sausage (about 4 links), diced
- 1 medium white onion, diced
- 12 large eggs
- 4 individual rolls, preferably *bolillos* or Portuguese rolls
- ½ cup hot Refried Black Beans (page 166)
- 4 pickled jalapeños, sliced
- 1 large ripe avocado, halved, pitted, peeled, and thinly sliced
- 1 tomato, thinly sliced
- 1 cup shredded iceberg lettuce
  Salt and freshly ground black pepper

Coat a large skillet with the 2 tablespoons of oil and heat over a medium flame. Add the chorizo and cook, stirring, for 5 minutes, until the sausage renders its fat and gets crispy. Mix in the onion and cook for 5 minutes, until soft. Beat the eggs in a small bowl until fluffy, then pour into the pan. Fold the eggs into the chorizo and onion, and cook for 5 to 8 minutes, until set.

Halve the rolls lengthwise. Brush the insides with a little oil and toast in a dry, hot skillet or under the broiler until golden.

To assemble the tortas, spread 2 tablespoons of the hot refried beans on the top halves of the rolls, add a sliced jalapeño, and press them into the beans using the back of a spoon. Line the bottom halves of the rolls with the sliced avocado and mash it into the bread. Add a couple of slices of tomato, some shredded lettuce, and a quarter of the egg mixture. Season with salt and pepper to taste and put the halves together.

GORDITAS

{corn flour patties}

It is nearly impossible to walk more than a block in any Mexican neighborhood in the United States without encountering a food vendor or two with a stand on the street. Even in Spanish Harlem in Manhattan, there is a community of women who sell freshly fried *gorditas* ("little fatties") from little carts on 116th Street. *Gorditas* are standard snack fare; the best way to make them is with your hands.

MAKES 1 DOZEN

> 2 cups *masa harina* (see Note, page 77)
> 1/4 cup all-purpose flour
> 1 teaspoon baking powder
> 1/2 teaspoon salt
> Canola oil for frying
> 1 1/2 cups Chicken Filling (recipe follows)
> 1/2 cup grated *queso Cotija* or *queso Añejo* (see Note)

Mix the *masa*, flour, baking powder, and salt in a large bowl. Gradually add 1 1/2 cups of warm water; you may need to add a little more to make a moist, smooth dough. Form the dough into walnut-size balls and cover with a damp towel as you work to prevent them from drying out.

Moisten a cloth napkin or tea towel and spread out on a flat surface. Roll each ball of dough in the moistened palm of your hand until smooth, lay one on the damp towel, cover with plastic wrap, and press down with your hand to flatten to the size of a silver dollar. To shape the patty, flatten it again with a small can or flat-bottomed glass into a perfectly smooth circle 2 to 2 1/2 inches in diameter and about 1/4 inch thick. Peel the plastic off, then lay the tortilla in your hand and peel away the damp cloth. Smooth any rough edges with your fingers and the patty is ready to fry. Repeat with the remaining balls of dough, keeping the patties covered with a towel as you work.

In a wide pot or deep skillet, heat 2 inches of oil to 375°F. (Check the temperature with an instant-read thermometer or sprinkle some *masa* in the hot oil; if it sizzles, the oil is ready.) Carefully slide the patties into the hot oil and fry until they are puffed and crisp, turning to brown evenly, about 5 minutes. Remove to a platter lined with paper towels to drain and sprinkle with salt to taste. Make a slit on the side of each *gordita* as soon as they are cool enough to handle. Stuff a couple of tablespoons of the chicken filling inside and garnish with grated cheese.

gorditas chicken filling

I grew up eating *gorditas* stuffed with chicken. This filling is very versatile: for a *torta* sandwich; folded into scrambled eggs; or just put 2 tablespoons in a corn tortilla, roll it up like a cigar, secure with toothpicks, and deep-fry to make *flautas*.

MAKES 2 CUPS

      3 tablespoons canola oil
      1 garlic clove, minced
    ½ cup canned chopped tomatoes, with juice
      3 scallions, white and green parts, chopped
      1 jalapeño, minced
  1½ cups shredded cooked chicken (page 226)
        Salt and freshly ground black pepper

In a large skillet, heat the oil over a medium flame until smoking. Add the garlic and cook until it just starts to turn golden, about 1 minute. Add the tomatoes, scallions, and jalapeño, and cook stirring, for 5 minutes. Add the shredded chicken, season with salt and pepper to taste, and cook for 5 minutes to combine the flavors.

QUESO COTIJA AND QUESO AÑEJO

Aged, strong-tasting, and somewhat hard and dry cheeses that are made from cow's milk. *Añejo* cheese is the aged version of *queso fresco*. *Cotija* cheese is named for the town of Cotija, Michoacán, where it originated. Called "the Parmesan of Mexico," they are ideal for grating.

SOPES

There is a saying that no Mexican table is complete without tortillas. *Sopes* are basically little boats of fried tortillas used as a canvas for salsas, cheeses, or black beans—good party food. Most street food and snacks are corn dough–based, and it's rumored that a typical Mexican eats a pound of corn per day. Look at the recipes in this chapter if you need more proof.

SERVES 10

1½ cups *masa harina* (see Note, page 77)
Canola oil for frying
Salt to taste
1½ cups Chorizo and Potato Filling (recipe follows)
½ cup chopped cilantro

Preheat a nonstick griddle over a medium flame and keep hot. Mix the *masa* with ¾ cup of warm water in a mixing bowl or electric mixer; you may need to add a little more to make a moist, smooth dough. Put the dough in a plastic bag to prevent it from drying out while you work. Pinch off walnut-size pieces of dough and roll them in the moistened palms of your hands until smooth. Place the dough between two pieces of plastic and press down with your hand to flatten to a thick patty about 2½ inches in diameter and ½ inch thick. Peel off the plastic and pinch up around the sides of the patties to form a little lip to hold the filling. Cook the patties on the hot griddle for 5 minutes on each side, turning once only, until the dough firms up. Remove to a plate.

In a wide pot or deep skillet, heat 2 inches of oil to 375°F. (Check the temperature with an instant-read thermometer or sprinkle some *masa* in the hot oil; if it sizzles, the oil is ready.) Carefully slide the patties into the hot oil and fry for 30 seconds, just to crisp up but not brown. Remove them to a platter lined with paper towels and sprinkle with salt. Put 2 tablespoons of the chorizo filling on each patty, top with 1 teaspoon cilantro, and serve.

sopes de chorizo and potato filling

You can make this filling a day in advance if you wish; be sure to reheat it before topping the *sopes*. Potato and chorizo is a familiar pairing that can be used in a variety of proportions: While it often accompanies eggs in the morning, I serve it stuffed in a quesadilla at my restaurant, Paladar.

MAKES 1 QUART

2 Idaho potatoes, peeled and diced
1 tablespoon salt
1 tablespoon canola oil
1 pound Spanish chorizo sausage (about 4 links), diced small (see Note, page 19)
1 medium white onion, diced
2 garlic cloves, minced
1 red bell pepper, cored and diced
1 yellow bell pepper, cored and diced
1 green bell pepper, cored and diced
1 cup Chicken Broth (page 227)
1 scallion, white and green parts, chopped
½ cup chopped cilantro
   Salt and freshly ground black pepper

Put the potatoes in a large pot and cover with cold water; add the salt and bring to a boil, uncovered. Simmer until fork-tender, about 15 minutes.

Meanwhile, coat a large skillet with the oil and heat over a medium flame. Add the chorizo and cook, stirring, for 5 minutes, until the sausage renders its fat and gets crispy. Add the onion, garlic, and all the peppers. Cook for 8 minutes, until the vegetables soften. Pour in the broth and simmer for 3 minutes. Drain the tender potatoes and add them to the pan, along with the scallion and cilantro. Cook for 3 more minutes to reduce the liquid, then season with salt and pepper to taste.

PUPUSAS

{stuffed corn turnovers}

Pupusas—El Salvador's national treasure—are corn tortillas stuffed with a variety of fillings, with cheese always included; my favorite is the simple duo of bean and cheese. *Pupusas* are stuffed before the dough is cooked, while flautas and burritos are stuffed after the dough is cooked—in Italian terms, *pupusas* are more like calzones than sandwiches. *Pupusas* are the main feature of Salvadoran restaurants, served alongside rice and beans to create a complete meal. This recipe is courtesy of my friend Ricardo Cordona in New York City.

MAKES 15

- 1 pound *masa harina* (see Note, page 77)
- 1/3 cup unsalted butter, melted
- 2 tablespoons lard (page 224)
- 1 medium white onion, chopped
- 1 cup Refried Black Beans (page 166)
- 1 cup grated *queso blanco* (see Note, page 75)
- Canola oil for brushing
- Salt
- Salsa or hot sauce

In a large bowl or electric mixer, combine the *masa harina*, melted butter, and 1 cup of warm water; you may need to add a little more water to make a moist, smooth dough. Cover and set aside.

Melt the lard in a skillet over medium heat. Add the onion and cook for 5 minutes, until soft. Add the refried beans and cook, stirring, for 5 minutes to combine and heat through. Remove from the heat.

Preheat a nonstick griddle over a medium flame and keep hot. Put the dough in a plastic bag to prevent it from drying out while you work. Pinch off walnut-size pieces of dough and roll them in the moistened palms of your hands until smooth. Place the balls of dough between two pieces of plastic and press down with your hand to flatten to a patty about 3 inches in diameter and up to 1/4 inch thick. Add 1 tablespoon of the bean filling and 1 tablespoon of the grated cheese in the center of a circle. Cap the filling with another corn-dough disc and pinch around the edges to form a tight seal. Brush both sides of the *pupusas* with oil and cook on the hot griddle for 5 minutes on each side, turning frequently, until browned. Sprinkle with salt and serve with your favorite salsa or hot sauce.

TORTA **MILANESA**

{breaded steak sandwich}

Mexican cooks adapted the Milan style of pounding and breading beef from the Italians. Top round is a relatively inexpensive cut of beef from the hind leg portion. I prefer making my own bread crumbs; pulsing day-old bread in a food processor is a simple task and the results are far superior to the stuff sold in the canister.

SERVES 4

1	pound top round steak
1	day-old baguette, crust on
½	cup all-purpose flour
1	tablespoon salt, plus more to taste
1	tablespoon freshly ground black pepper, plus more to taste
1	large egg
¼	cup whole milk
2	tablespoons extra-virgin olive oil, plus more for brushing the rolls
4	individual rolls, preferably *bolillos* or Portuguese rolls
½	cup hot Refried Black Beans (page 166)
4	pickled jalapeños, sliced
1	large ripe avocado, halved, pitted, peeled, and thinly sliced
1	tomato, thinly sliced
1	cup shredded iceberg lettuce

Using a sharp knife, cut the steak into ½-inch-thick slices. Place the slices between two pieces of plastic wrap and pound with the smooth side of a mallet into ⅛-inch-thick medallions. Transfer to a platter and set aside.

To make the bread crumbs, preheat the oven to 200°F. Using a serrated knife, cut the semistale bread into chunks, spread out on a sheet pan, and bake for 10 minutes, until dry but not toasted like croutons. Transfer the bread to a food processor and pulse until ground into coarse crumbs; spread the bread crumbs on a plate.

On another plate, combine the flour with 1 tablespoon each of salt and pepper; mix with your fingers to distribute evenly. In a small bowl, whisk the egg and milk together until frothy.

Coat a skillet with the 2 tablespoons of oil and place over medium heat. Dredge each steak slice in the flour, dip in the egg wash, then coat in the bread crumbs; both sides should be well covered. Fry the breaded steak in the hot oil for 2 minutes on each side, until the coating becomes a golden crust. Remove to a platter lined with paper towels as they are ready.

Halve the rolls lengthwise. Brush the insides with a little oil and toast in a dry, hot skillet or under the broiler until golden.

To assemble the *tortas*, spread 2 tablespoons of the hot refried beans on the top halves of the rolls, add a sliced jalapeño, and press into the beans with the back of a spoon. Line the bottom halves of the rolls with the sliced avocado and mash it into the bread. Add a couple of slices of tomato, some shredded lettuce, and a few slices of the fried steak. Season with salt and pepper to taste and put the halves together.

CROQUETAS DE **JAMÓN**

{ham croquettes}

Croquetas were brought over by the Cubans who settled in Florida. They are often sold in bakeries as snacks. At the famous Versailles restaurant in the heart of Miami's Little Havana, besides finding great Cuban coffee and pastries, you'll find these croquettes in a warm glass case ready to be plucked from their resting place. They're great finger food and perfect for parties.

SERVES 4

2 tablespoons canola oil, plus more for panfrying

2 pounds cured ham, cubed

1 medium white onion, diced

2 red bell peppers, cored and diced

1 jalapeño, minced

¼ teaspoon freshly grated nutmeg

2 tablespoons chopped flat-leaf parsley, plus more for garnish

½ cup all-purpose flour, plus more for dusting

½ cup tomato paste

1 cup whole milk

Salt and freshly ground black pepper

2 large eggs, beaten

2 cups cracker meal or dried fine bread crumbs

2 lemons, cut in wedges, for serving

Heat the 2 tablespoons of oil in a large skillet over a medium flame. Add the ham, onion, peppers, jalapeño, nutmeg, and 2 tablespoons of parsley; cook until caramelized, about 10 minutes.

Sprinkle in ¼ cup of the flour and stir for 1 minute to cook out the raw taste and incorporate. In a small bowl, combine the tomato paste and the milk; whisk to dilute the paste and smooth out the lumps. Add this mixture to the skillet, season with salt and pepper to taste, and cook, stirring, for 5 minutes to form a thick, creamy sauce. Remove from the heat and let cool for 5 minutes.

Scrape the ham mixture into a food processor and pulse to a coarse paste; it should have a doughy consistency. Put the ham mixture on a sheet pan, spread out evenly, and chill in the refrigerator for 2 hours, so it will be easy to roll.

Put the remaining ¼ cup of flour in a small bowl and dust the counter generously with flour. In another bowl, beat the eggs until frothy. Put the cracker meal in yet another bowl.

Divide the dough into thirds. Using your hands, roll each piece of dough into a cylinder about 1 foot long and ¾ inch thick. Using a knife, cut the cylinders into finger-size logs about 2 inches long. Dredge the logs in the flour; dip them in the egg wash, letting the excess drip off, and roll them in the cracker meal. Put the breaded croquettes in the refrigerator for 10 minutes to set the coating.

In a wide pot or deep skillet, heat 1 inch of oil to 375°F. (Check the temperature with an instant-read thermometer or sprinkle some flour in the hot oil; if it sizzles, the oil is ready.) Fry the croquettes, a few at a time, carefully rotating them so they brown evenly, about 3 minutes. Remove and drain on a paper towel–lined plate. Season with salt and pepper to taste while hot, and serve with lemon wedges, garnished with parsley.

PAN CON **LECHÓN**

These sandwiches are one of the favorites of my dear friend and fellow chef Alex García, a Cuban who could have them at any time of day. The recipe again utilizes leftover meat from when Cuban families make *pernil* or *lechón asado*. Pickled red onions are a familiar condiment in Cuban eateries. Electric sandwich presses are used to compress and heat the sandwich, much like *panini;* at home, a waffle iron or a hot griddle coupled with a weighty object will also provide success. Seek out Cuban bread to make this and the Sandwich Cubano (page 103) recipe. If you have no alternative, substitute bread that is somewhat crusty on the outside and soft in the middle, such as French rolls, but *never* use a baguette, which is too narrow and hard to press correctly.

SERVES 4

2 tablespoons canola oil

2 red onions, thinly sliced

Juice of 2 limes

½ teaspoon salt

¼ teaspoon freshly ground black pepper

4 individual Cuban or French rolls

6 tablespoons unsalted butter, at room temperature, plus more for the griddle

2 cups shredded pork, such as *pernil* or *lechón asado* (pages 118 and 119)

Heat the oil in a large skillet over a medium flame. Add the red onions and cook, stirring, until soft, about 5 minutes. Pour in the lime juice and continue to cook until the juice is absorbed. Season with the salt and pepper to taste.

To make the sandwiches, cut the rolls in half lengthwise, leaving the halves attached like a hinge. Spread 1 tablespoon of butter on the insides. Add ½ cup of pork and a couple of tablespoons of the pickled onions; press the sandwich together. Place a griddle over very low heat and add a little butter. Put the sandwiches in the pan and weigh them down with a can or heavy pot to flatten (use a brick wrapped in foil if nothing else is available). Cook for 3 to 5 minutes on each side, but make sure the bread does not burn. Slice the sandwiches in half on a diagonal.

CROQUETAS DE **PESCADO**

{fish croquettes}

Originally from Spain, now eaten all over Cuba, this dish is a great example of using leftover fish scraps to create something that can be enjoyed at all times of the day.

SERVES 4

2 tablespoons canola oil, plus more for panfrying

2 pounds scrod, hake, or cod, chopped

1 medium white onion, diced

1 carrot, diced

1 celery stalk, diced

1 red bell pepper, cored and diced

1 green bell pepper, cored and diced

1 tablespoon freshly grated ginger

1 teaspoon salt

1 teaspoon freshly ground black pepper

½ cup soy sauce

¼ cup (½ stick) unsalted butter

½ cup all-purpose flour, plus more for dusting

1 cup whole milk

2 large eggs, lightly beaten

2 cups cracker meal or dried fine bread crumbs

2 lemons, cut in wedges, for serving

Flat-leaf parsley, for garnish

Heat 2 tablespoons of oil in a large skillet over a medium flame. Add the fish, onion, carrot, celery, peppers, and ginger; cook for 5 minutes, until soft. Season with the salt and pepper, add the soy sauce, and stir to evaporate. Remove from the heat and let cool for 5 minutes, then transfer to a food processor and pulse to a coarse paste.

In a large skillet, melt the butter over medium-low heat. When foamy, stir in ¼ cup of flour to make a roux. Whisk for about 1 minute to cook out the raw taste of the flour. Gradually pour in the milk, whisking the entire time to prevent lumps and to form a thick, creamy sauce.

Fold the fish mixture into the sauce. Mix well and cook for 4 to 5 minutes over medium-low heat to incorporate; it should have a doughy, pastelike consistency. Put the mixture on a sheet pan, spread out evenly, and chill in the refrigerator for 2 hours so it will be easy to handle.

Put the remaining ¼ cup of flour in a small bowl and dust the counter generously with flour. In another bowl, beat the eggs until frothy. Put the cracker meal in yet another bowl.

Divide the dough into thirds. Using your hands, roll each piece of dough into a cylinder about 1 foot long and ¾ inch thick. Using a knife, cut the cylinders into finger-size logs about 2 inches long. Roll the logs in the flour; dip them in the egg wash, letting the excess drip off, and roll them in the cracker meal. Put the breaded croquettes in the refrigerator for 10 minutes to set the coating.

In a wide pot or deep skillet, heat 1 inch of oil to 375°F. (Check the temperature with an instant-read thermometer or sprinkle some flour in the hot oil; if it sizzles, the oil is ready.) Fry the croquettes, a few at a time, carefully rotating them so they brown evenly, about 3 minutes. Remove and drain on a paper towel–lined plate. Season with salt and pepper to taste while hot, and serve with lemon wedges, garnished with parsley.

ANTICUCHOS DE **POLLO**

{grilled chicken skewers}

In Peru, *anticuchos* translates to "skewered meats," usually chicken livers and hearts; I've updated it by using chicken breast. These are always served with *ají verde* (page 235), a condiment that's on every Peruvian table. You will need 20 wooden skewers to make this recipe; remember to soak the sticks in water for 20 minutes to prevent them from burning.

MAKES 20
SERVES 10

½   cup chopped cilantro
½   cup chopped flat-leaf parsley
     Finely grated zest of 1 lemon
 6   garlic cloves, minced
½   cup extra-virgin olive oil, plus more for panfrying
1½   pounds skinless, boneless chicken breasts, cut into bite-size pieces

In a large mixing bowl, combine the cilantro, parsley, lemon zest, garlic, and oil. Add the chicken, toss to coat, cover, and marinate in the refrigerator for 1 hour.

Place a grill pan over medium heat and brush it with a little oil to prevent the meat from sticking. Thread the chicken pieces onto the soaked skewers (see headnote). Grill for 4 minutes on each side, until nicely seared and cooked through. Serve with your favorite hot sauce or *ají verde* (page 235).

SANDWICH **CUBANO**

{cuban sandwich}

This delicious sandwich is a classic Cuban lunch. The same filling ingredients are also used on a smaller, sweeter variety of bread and called a *medianoche*, or "midnight" sandwich, served cold and as a midnight snack after a movie or dancing. Thinly sliced roasted pork loin is commonly used in place of the *pernil* or *lechón*. I find that loin is too lean and does not provide enough juices to moisten and flavor the sandwich. Take the ingredients out of the refrigerator 20 minutes before grilling the sandwich so the meat and cheese are not too cold, and you'll avoid burning the bread before the cheese melts and the pork heats through; this is especially true when you pile a lot of meat on your sandwich like I do.

SERVES 4

4 individual Cuban or French rolls
1/4 cup golden mustard
1 cup sliced dill pickles
1/2 pound sliced Swiss cheese
1 pound smoked ham, sliced paper-thin
2 cups shredded pork, such as *pernil* or *lechón asado* (pages 118 and 119)
1/4 cup (1/2 stick) unsalted butter

To make the sandwiches, cut the rolls in half lengthwise, leaving the halves attached like a hinge. Spread 1 tablespoon of the mustard on the top side of each roll, then lay a quarter of the pickles on top of the mustard, followed by a quarter of the cheese. Divide the ham and pork among the bottom halves of the rolls and press the sandwich together.

Place a griddle over very low heat and add the butter. Put the sandwiches in the pan and weigh them down with a can or heavy pot to flatten (use a brick wrapped in foil if nothing else is available). Cook for 3 to 5 minutes on each side, until the cheese is melted and the bread is toasted and slightly crisp; make sure the bread does not burn. Slice the sandwiches in half on a diagonal.

CHICHARRÓNES

Pork cracklin's are the snack of choice for low-carb dieters, because they're high in protein and have zero carbohydrates. In Mexico, they are sold on the street in paper bags to soak up the grease. Ask your butcher for 1 inch of fat from the pork belly, trimming any visible pieces of meat. Pork rind is basically the fatty edges of bacon.

MAKES 12 PIECES
SERVES 6

2 pounds pork skin
2 tablespoons salt, plus more to taste
   Lard for frying (page 224)
2 teaspoons cayenne
1 lime, halved

Rub the pork skin on both sides with the salt, cover with plastic wrap, and let sit for 1 hour to pull out the moisture. Cut the pork skin into 2-inch-long and ½-inch-thick pieces.

In a wide pot or deep skillet, heat 3 inches of lard to 375°F. (Check the temperature with an instant-read thermometer or sprinkle some flour in the hot oil; if it sizzles, the oil is ready.) Fry the pork rinds, a few at a time, until puffed, golden, and crispy, about 5 to 10 minutes. Remove and drain on paper towels. Season with cayenne and additional salt to taste while they're still hot. Give a squeeze of lime juice before serving.

ALCAPURRÍAS

These tasty little dumplings are basically fritters stuffed with *picadillo*. The starchy plantains and yautia (a tuber) form a *masa*-like dough that fries up nicely. The classic salty-sweet trio of green olives, capers, and raisins is common in fillings for tamales, empanadas, or, in this case, *alcapurrías*. This is a popular summer dish in Puerto Rico, where it is often cooked on the beach; the dumplings are sometimes stuffed with crab or *bacalao*.

SERVES 6

5 green plantains, peeled (see Note, page 55)
1 pound yautia or sweet potato, peeled (see Note)
2 tablespoons warm lard (page 224)
2 tablespoons extra-virgin olive oil
1/2 pound ground beef
1 medium white onion, diced
2 garlic cloves, minced
1 red bell pepper, cored and diced
1 *cubanella* or green bell pepper, cored and diced (see Note, page 43)
1 ripe tomato, diced
1 teaspoon ground cumin
1 teaspoon ground coriander
1/2 teaspoon ground cloves
2 cups Beef Stock (page 230)
1/2 cup tomato paste
1/4 cup sliced green olives
2 tablespoons capers, drained
1/4 cup golden raisins
Salt and freshly ground black pepper
Canola oil for frying

Using a box grater, grate the plantains and yautia into a large mixing bowl. Pour in the lard, mix well, and set aside. This will be your dough.

Prepare the stuffing: In a large Dutch oven or skillet, heat the olive oil over a medium flame. When the oil begins to smoke, add the ground beef and spread it out evenly with a spatula or wooden spoon so it covers the entire bottom of the pan. Fry for 5 minutes without stirring so a nice crust forms. Add the onion, garlic, peppers, tomato, cumin, coriander, and cloves. Cook, stirring, for 15 minutes, until the vegetables soften and the spices are thoroughly incorporated.

In a mixing bowl, combine the stock and tomato paste and whisk to dilute the paste and smooth out any lumps; add to the beef mixture and simmer over medium heat for 10 minutes. Fold in the olives, capers, and raisins, mix well, and season with salt and pepper to taste. Remove from the heat and set aside to cool.

In a wide pot or deep skillet, heat 2 inches of canola oil to 375°F. (Check the temperature with an instant-read thermometer or sprinkle some flour in the hot oil; if it sizzles, the oil is ready.) Moisten your hands with water and grab about ¼ cup of the plantain-yautia dough. Use your other hand to flatten the dough into a ¼-inch-thick disc. Spoon 1 generous tablespoon of the filling into the center of the dough and fold it over in half to enclose the filling and form a semicircle. Seal the edges by crimping with the tines of a fork. Carefully drop the *alcapurrías* into the hot oil, one at a time, and fry for 5 minutes, turning occasionally to ensure that they are evenly browned. Remove to a plate lined with paper towels and season with additional salt and pepper while they are still hot.

YAUTIA

A tuber that is white, red, or yellow — any color will do for this recipe. It tastes like potatoes with flesh that is milky and starchy.

{the café: roasted meats}

BOLICHE
{cuban pot roast}

CARNE CON CHILE COLORADO
{steak in red chile sauce}

PICADILLO
{ground beef hash}

PERNIL AL HORNO
{roasted pork shoulder}

LECHÓN ASADO
{whole suckling pig}

CABRITO EN ADOBO
{adobo-rubbed baby goat}

BISTEC DE PALOMILLA
{butterflied steak}

MOLE DE POLLO
{chicken mole}

THROUGHOUT LATIN AMERICA, the climate is

pretty warm most of the year, if not unbearably hot. Outdoor cooking and eating are a big part of life, and that's something we bring to the barrio—not just as a backyard-barbecue, Fourth-of-July thing, as a regular event every month that it's possible, and year-round in the Latin strongholds of Florida, the border, and California.

When Latins cook outdoors, meat is the focus. Sometimes really huge pieces of meat are roasted: a side of beef, a pork shoulder, an entire baby goat or suckling pig, a bunch of birds. This requires a lot of space, and creates a lot of smoke and flame. It also requires a lot of people—a small family isn't going to knock off a suckling pig in an evening. Enter the *rotisería,* a restaurant (or a part of a restaurant) whose menu revolves around cooking anything (especially large cuts) that can be thrown on a grill. The typical *rotisería* has a backyard area for cooking, and a patio where people eat. The patio is often rented out for large private parties—brunches, weddings, birthdays—that need the space and the impressive quantity of food.

The meats themselves usually depend on a marinade for an infusion of flavor, and most of the dishes are served with a side of sauce—a mojo or salsa—to provide an additional burst of spice and juiciness. Typically, the *rotisería* also offers its grilled meats to go: You get a pound or two of their *pernil asado,* take it home to the family with some bread, and make your own sandwiches; Mexican-Americans are thrilled to take home some roasted goat by the pound. This is the perfect arrangement if you're not feeding an army but still want a cut of meat that typically comes in 10-pound segments.

The recipes in this chapter are scaled down for the home kitchen and are practical to make at home. Admittedly, "practical" is a matter of judgment, and some people may disagree that a suckling pig or baby goat is something they want to drag into their homes and shove into their ovens. But if you're one of those adventurous souls who take my side of this argument, the recipes are in here. Big cuts, with big flavor.

BOLICHE

{cuban pot roast}

Cuba was colonized by the Spanish. This history gives Cuban food a distinct combination of European, African, and Caribbean influences. Cuban dishes are highly seasoned, but not spicy. Familiar flavors like garlic, oregano, onion, and green peppers are mixed with the unusual, such as bitter orange, which infuses the cooking with a piquant taste that doesn't overwhelm and is distinctly Cuban.

The West Tampa area of Florida has a large Cuban population and the most Cuban-run businesses outside of Dade County. The hub of the community is Columbus Drive, affectionately nicknamed "Boliche Boulevard"; the area lies just south of the stadium and boasts a profusion of Cuban restaurants, bakeries, and markets. There are also cigar factories, flower shops, and *botánicas*—shops that sell the potions used in Afro-Cuban Santeria rituals. *Boliche* is a yummy stuffed roast, and you can find it, and much more Cuban food, anywhere on Columbus. The name also refers to the cut of meat—often beef eye round is referred to simply as *boliche*. The slow cooking of this dish is a great way to turn a poorer cut into a delicious feast—moist and tender.

SERVES 4 TO 6

8 garlic cloves, smashed

1 teaspoon cumin seeds

1 teaspoon dried Mexican oregano (see Note, page 73)

1 teaspoon salt

1/2 teaspoon coarsely ground black pepper

1 boneless beef eye round roast (4 to 5 pounds), trimmed

1 pound ham, cubed

   Juice of 8 Seville oranges (about 1 cup; see Note, page 83)

1/4 cup canola oil

1 onion, coarsely chopped

2 green bell peppers, cored and coarsely chopped

1 15-ounce can tomato purée

1 cup dry sherry

   Cooked white rice, for serving

Using a mortar and pestle, mash the garlic, cumin, oregano, salt, and pepper into a paste. With a sharp knife, slice the beef round lengthwise down the center to make a pocket. Rub the garlic paste inside and all over the roast. Stuff the cavity of the beef with the ham cubes, then press the incision together to close it up. Put the meat on a platter and pour the orange juice over it. Cover and refrigerate at least 3 hours or up to overnight.

Preheat the oven to 350°F.

Remove the meat from the marinade and reserve the liquid. Heat the oil in a large Dutch oven or other ovenproof pot over a medium-high flame. When the oil begins to smoke, lay the roast in the pan and sear on all sides. Add the onion, peppers, tomato purée, sherry, and reserved marinade. Bring up to a boil, cover, and transfer to the oven to roast for 2 hours.

Remove the beef to a cutting board and let it rest for 10 minutes to allow the juices to settle, then slice it up. Serve the pot roast with white rice and some pan sauce poured over the top.

CARNE CON CHILE COLORADO

This dish originated in northern Mexico, where cattle ranches are prevalent. Flank steak and brisket are the most common cuts of beef used here because they are inexpensive and can be easily shredded. Slow cooking infuses the smoky chili sauce into the meat.

SERVES 4

1	tablespoon ground cumin
1	tablespoon ground coriander
1	tablespoon mustard seed, smashed
3/4	cup extra-virgin olive oil, plus more for coating the pan
3	teaspoons salt, plus more to taste
3	teaspoons freshly ground black pepper, plus more to taste
2	pounds flank steak, trimmed of excess fat
1/2	pound *guajillo* chiles, stemmed and seeded (see Note, page 121)
1/2	pound *ancho* chiles, stemmed and seeded (see Note, page 49)
1	small white onion, peeled and halved
8	garlic cloves, peeled
4	medium tomatillos, husked and rinsed
2	large tomatoes, halved
	Corn tortillas
1/4	cup shredded Jack cheese

Place a small dry skillet over medium-low heat and toast the cumin, coriander, and mustard for 1 minute, until fragrant, shaking the pan so they don't scorch. Put the toasted spices in a small bowl, add 1/2 cup of the oil and 1 teaspoon each salt and pepper, and mix to make a paste. Rub the paste on both sides of the flank steak, cover, and marinate in the refrigerator for 1 hour.

Bring 3 cups of water to a boil. In a dry cast-iron skillet, toast the *guajillo* and *ancho* chiles over medium-low heat for 2 minutes, until fragrant; turn them and shake the pan so they don't scorch. Put the toasted chiles in a bowl, cover with the boiling water, and let soak until softened and reconstituted, about 20 minutes.

Return the skillet to a medium-high flame and let it get nice and hot, a good 2 minutes. Rub the onion, garlic, tomatillos, and tomatoes with the remaining 1/4 cup of oil. Lay the vegetables in the hot pan and roast, turning occasionally, until soft and well charred on all sides, about 10 minutes. Put the vegetables in a bowl to let them cool a bit, then coarsely chop. Put them in a blender with the chiles and their soaking water, and purée until completely smooth (you will have to do this in batches). Season with additional salt and pepper to taste.

Preheat the oven to 350°F.

Preheat a ridged grill pan over a medium-high flame. Brush the pan with a little oil to prevent the meat from sticking. Season the steak on both sides with the remaining 2 teaspoons each of salt and pepper, and grill for 3 minutes per side; it will not be fully cooked. Transfer to a baking pan, pour the puréed sauce over it, and cover with foil. Bake for 1 hour, until the meat is very tender and falling apart. Allow the steak to cool slightly, then hand-shred.

To serve, put a small amount of shredded meat on a warm corn tortilla, add a spoonful of the red sauce, and top with the shredded cheese. Put the tortillas on a sheet pan and return to the oven for 5 minutes to melt the cheese and brown slightly.

SANDY'S PUERTO RICAN

Sandy's façade is misleading: The window display filled with fried food makes it look as if you'll have a heart attack just by walking in. But inside, you'll find a wide selection that includes some non-fried items, including my favorites: *pernil asada* (marinated pork shoulder), *lechón asado* (whole roasted pig), *guajito* (pickled green plantains), *pasteles* (a combination of pureed tubers with braised pork wrapped in banana leaves and boiled), and *alcapurrías* (fried stuffed plantains). There are also cooling octopus and shrimp cocktails and ceviches, as well as a variety of awesome *batidos* (shakes). Finish the meal with one of their great coffees, like the Cuban version, made with an espresso machine.

Sandy's is a real New York joint, a place to visit as much for the music and people as for the food. The first thing you see when you walk in, in fact, is a huge counterspace with lots of staff ready to attend to your every need. This, I thought, would make a great location for a spot of Food Network's *Melting Pot,* so I took my on-air partner, Alex, for lunch. The place was full of cops— there must have been six or seven, all Latin, catching a quick taste of home. We asked the owners if we could film on premises, and they were reluctant. But Alex spread around some of his charm, and ended up behind the counter, wearing a white hat and serving food, and they came around. A few days later, we arrived with the crew and filmed the flavor of the barrio.

PICADILLO

Picadillo comes from the Spanish verb *picar*, "to chop into small pieces," but it is often used as a loose term for a mixture of ground meat and spices, much like American hash. This skillet dish is a favorite in many Latin-American countries, especially Cuba, and is also a favorite filling for Mexican chiles rellenos and empanadas.

SERVES 4 TO 6

- 1 tablespoon extra-virgin olive oil
- 2 pounds ground beef
- 1 medium white onion, chopped
- 3 garlic cloves, minced
- 1 *cubanella* or green bell pepper, cored and diced (see Note, page 43)
- 1 canned *chipotle* in adobo, chopped (see Note, page 71)
- 3 bay leaves
- 1 teaspoon ground cumin
- 1 tablespoon dried Mexican oregano (see Note, page 73)
  Salt and freshly ground black pepper
- 1 6-ounce can tomato paste
- 1 tablespoon sherry vinegar
- 1/2 cup sliced pimiento-stuffed green olives
- 1/4 cup toasted sliced almonds
- 1/4 cup golden raisins
- 1/4 cup chopped fresh flat-leaf parsley

In a large skillet or Dutch oven, heat the oil over a medium flame. When the oil begins to smoke, add the ground beef and spread it out evenly with a spatula or wooden spoon so it covers the entire bottom of the pan. Fry for 5 minutes without stirring so a nice crust forms. As the meat begins to lose its red tint, start mixing in the onion, garlic, pepper, *chipotle*, bay leaves, cumin, and oregano. Season with salt and pepper to taste and let it cook for 8 minutes, until the vegetables are soft.

In a small bowl, combine the tomato paste with 1 cup of warm water. Whisk to dilute the tomato paste and smooth out the lumps, then add it to the pot. Add the vinegar and fold in the olives, almonds, and raisins; give everything a good stir to incorporate. Shower with the chopped parsley and serve.

PERNIL AL **HORNO**

{roasted pork shoulder}

Pernil is about as Latin as you can get, sold in eateries by the pound. I try to go down to Miami every March for the Calle Ocho festival—the smell of slow-roasted pork wafting through the air just gets my blood pumping.

The Cuban peasant style of cooking is simple in concept but complex in flavor. Here, pork is rubbed with salt to pull out the juices and help form a crust on the meat when cooked. Serve with Yellow Rice and Dominican-Style Red Beans (pages 158 and 162). The leftover pork is perfect for the Cuban Sandwich and *Pan con Lechón* (pages 103 and 99).

SERVES 10 TO 12

1 boneless pork shoulder (about 5 pounds), trimmed of excess fat

3 garlic cloves, smashed

1 tablespoon dried Mexican oregano (see Note, page 73)

5 tablespoons kosher salt

1 tablespoon coarsely ground black pepper

3 tablespoons extra-virgin olive oil

Place the pork, fat-side up, in a roasting pan fitted with a rack insert. Using a sharp knife, score the surface of the meat with small slits. Using a mortar and pestle, mash the garlic, oregano, salt, pepper, and oil into a paste. Rub the garlic paste all over the pork, being sure to get in the incisions so the salt can penetrate the meat and pull out the moisture. Cover the pork with plastic wrap and marinate in the refrigerator overnight or up to 24 hours.

Remove the pork from the refrigerator and allow it to sit at room temperature for 30 minutes before cooking.

Preheat the oven to 350°F.

Roast the pork for 2½ hours, or 30 minutes per pound; the outside of the meat should have a nice crust and the internal temperature should be 155°F. Let rest for 10 minutes before slicing.

LECHÓN ASADO

{whole suckling pig}

In Cuba, Puerto Rico, and the Dominican Republic, this dish is traditionally served at large open-air parties. As in the Hawaiian luau, the pig is covered with banana leaves and cooked over hot coals in a pit that's dug in the ground. Because this method is not easy at home, use a small suckling pig that will fit in the oven yet deliver the same slow-barbecued flavor. The pig should be well washed and eviscerated. Frequent basting in *achiote* oil adds a golden red color and crisps the skin. Serve with the garlic-vinegar condiment *Ají-li-Mójili* (page 232) and Cuban Black Beans and Rice (page 159).

1 medium white onion, coarsely chopped

6 garlic cloves, coarsely chopped

1/2 cup coarsely chopped fresh cilantro

Juice of 16 Seville oranges (about 2 cups; see Note, page 83)

2 cups white vinegar

1 tablespoon dried Mexican oregano (see Note, page 73)

1 tablespoon ground cumin

2 bay leaves

1 tablespoon salt

1 tablespoon freshly ground black pepper

1 whole suckling pig (about 12 to 15 pounds)

1 1/2 cups *achiote* oil (page 225)

In a blender, combine the onion, garlic, cilantro, orange juice, vinegar, oregano, cumin, bay leaves, salt, and pepper; purée until smooth. Lay the pig in a large, deep roasting pan, head up (put it in a large plastic bag if you don't have a large enough pan). Using a sharp knife, make small slits all over the skin. Pour the marinade over the pork and massage it into the incisions as well as inside the cavity. Cover and refrigerate overnight, turning occasionally.

Remove all the racks but the bottom one of your oven and preheat it to 300°F.

Remove the pig from the marinade and cover the ears, snout, and tail with aluminum foil to prevent them from burning. Roast for 6 to 7 hours, or 30 minutes per pound, until the inner thigh reads 155°F. Baste every hour with the oil. Let the pig rest for 15 to 20 minutes before carving.

CABRITO EN ADOBO

{adobo-rubbed baby goat}

When I was growing up in El Paso, my father had a fifty-gallon drum dug into the ground in our backyard for the sole purpose of cooking large cuts of meat slowly in a marinade, or *adobo*, of different chiles. This dish, also referred to as *barbacoa de cabrito* (barbecued goat), has roots in the Mexican states of Sonora and Jalisco. People commonly dig pits in the ground, heat large stones, add the meat, cover it with leaves, and cook it in the ground for up to a full day. If goat is not your thing, substitute lamb.

SERVES 12

  5 pounds baby goat shoulder (see Note)

  1/2 pound *guajillo* chiles, stemmed and seeded (see Note)

  1/2 pound *ancho* chiles, stemmed and seeded (see Note, page 49)

  1/2 pound *pasilla* chiles, stemmed and seeded (see Note)

  5 whole allspice berries

  3 whole cloves

  6 garlic cloves, minced

  2 tablespoons dried Mexican oregano (see Note, page 73)

  1/4 cup white vinegar

  1/2 cup extra-virgin olive oil

  1 tablespoon salt

  1 tablespoon freshly ground black pepper

  1 pound package banana leaves (see Note)

  6 dried avocado leaves (see Note)

With a sharp knife, score both sides of the goat shoulder with 1/4-inch-wide incisions and set aside.

Bring 1 quart of water to a boil and place over a large bowl. In a dry heavy skillet, preferably cast-iron, add the *guajillo* chiles over medium-low heat. Toast for 1 minute on each side, until they start to release aroma and smoke, then immediately submerge them in the bowl of boiling water. Let the chiles steep for 15 minutes, until they are soft and pliable. Using a slotted spoon, remove them from the water and set aside. Repeat the process with the *ancho* and *pasilla* chiles.

Using the same skillet, toast the allspice and cloves for 2 minutes, shaking the pan so they do not scorch. Put the spices in a clean coffee grinder or spice mill and grind to a powder. In a food processor, purée the drained chiles. Add them to a large bowl along with the garlic, oregano, vinegar, oil, and spice powder; mix well to combine.

Season both sides of the goat shoulder with the salt and pepper. Add the meat to the chile marinade, turning to coat both sides. Cover the bowl with plastic wrap and put it in the refrigerator for at least 8 hours or up to overnight.

Preheat the oven to 350°F.

Lay half of the banana leaves on a rack fitted inside a large roasting pan; you want the leaves to completely cover the bottom of the pan so the meat is insulated. Place the goat on top of the banana leaves and distribute the avocado leaves all over the top. Cover with the remaining banana leaves, making sure the meat is completely covered. Cover the roasting pan tightly with aluminum foil and roast for 2½ hours, until the meat is tender and falling off the bone.

GOAT SHOULDER

A delicate meat that tastes similar to lamb. The best time to buy really young *cabrito* is from May through October; after that they get too old and mutton-tasting. Texans are big fans of barbecuing goat.

GUAJILLO CHILE

The dried form of the fresh *mirasol* chile. Commonly used to give sauces and marinades a bright red color, it is ferociously hot and is called *travieso* ("mischievous") in parts of Mexico because of its bite.

PASILLA CHILE

Literally translated as "little raisin," the dried form of the fresh *chilaca*. This black chile with wrinkled skin has a deep, sharp flavor with a medium-hot spiciness.

AVOCADO LEAVES

Have an aniselike, herbaceous flavor.

BANANA LEAVES

Generally used for steaming because they impart a grassy-green flavor to the food wrapped inside. By and large, banana leaves are sold frozen in Latin and Asian markets; they are difficult to find fresh.

BISTEC DE **PALOMILLA**

This Cuban-style pounded steak is simply incredible; I had this on the menu when I was executive chef at L-Ray in Greenwich Village. The combination of pounding the meat and marinating it in acidic lime juice results in tender, juicy steak that you can cut with a fork; the marinade is great with any of your favorite steaks. Serve with *Papas Chorreadas* (page 172).

SERVES 12

Juice of 4 limes

2 tablespoons chopped fresh oregano

1 teaspoon ground cumin

3 garlic cloves, minced

6 tablespoons extra-virgin olive oil, plus more for coating the pan

1 boneless beef eye roast (4 to 5 pounds), trimmed of excess fat

2 medium white onions, thinly sliced

1/4 cup chopped fresh flat-leaf parsley

Salt

Freshly ground black pepper

In a small bowl, combine the lime juice, oregano, cumin, garlic, and 4 tablespoons of the oil.

Using a sharp knife, cut the eye roast into 1/2-inch-thick slices. Place the slices between two pieces of plastic wrap and pound with a mallet into 1/4-inch-thick medallions. Put the medallions in a baking pan, pour the marinade over, cover, and marinate for 1 hour in the refrigerator.

Place a skillet over medium heat and coat with the remaining 2 tablespoons of oil. Add the onions and cook, stirring, for 20 minutes, until caramelized. Add the parsley, season with salt and pepper to taste, remove from the heat, and set aside.

Preheat a ridged grill pan over a medium-high flame. Brush the pan with a little oil to prevent the meat from sticking. Season the beef medallions on both sides with 1 tablespoon each of salt and pepper, and grill for 3 minutes per side; the pieces will cook quickly because they are so thin. Serve with the reserved onions.

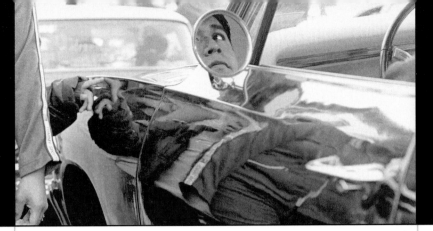

As everyone knows, soccer is the national sport of almost every nation on earth, and certainly of all the countries in Latin America. So it's no surprise that it's also the sport of choice in the barrio, whether it's just kicking the ball in the street or a full-team, full-field, full-uniform refereed affair under lights on a Saturday night. From New York City's Red Hook to Flushing Park, from the FDR Drive to Randall's Island, you can witness the strong sense of community by dropping by a neighborhood game.

And one of the remarkable things you'll notice is that this is a totally well-executed nonprofessional sports match, played by *adults*—this isn't Little League. You need twenty or thirty guys, in good shape with decent skills, who are willing to practice regularly and spend their free time running around a field, kicking a ball. Where do you see a nine-on-nine hardball baseball game, with coaches and umpires and uniforms, played a full nine innings by skilled players? In a stadium, where you buy tickets for assigned seats, that's where. But *fútbol* is in the public park around the corner.

Another remarkable thing is the food—street vendors offering *tacos de carne asada, tortas,* tamales, *gorditas, sopes.* Mango with chile and lime, corn with spicy mayonnaise. All washed down with Coronas and Jarrittos (fruit sodas), and all much less expensive than you'd expect—a soccer match in a public park offers one of the best eating values in the country. (And if you're ever lucky enough to go to a sporting match in Mexico, don't miss the concessions, where you're likely to find hot dogs with jalapeños and hamburgers with avocado).

There are families having picnics, teenagers checking each other out, old people sitting in folding chairs watching the game. Music is blaring from boom boxes, young men are admiring cars, little kids are running around screaming. It's a rich park culture, in a family environment that also includes adult fun. It's a real authentic slice of the homeland, with a sports match to boot. Try it sometime.

MOLE DE **POLLO**

{chicken mole}

½ pound *guajillo* chiles, stemmed and seeded (see Note, page 121)

½ pound *pasilla* chiles, stemmed and seeded (see Note, page 121)

½ pound *ancho* chiles, stemmed and seeded (see Note, page 49)

1 medium white onion, peeled and quartered

8 garlic cloves, peeled

3 large ripe tomatoes, quartered

10 small tomatillos, husked and rinsed

½ cup extra-virgin olive oil

1 teaspoon cumin seeds

1 teaspoon fennel seeds

1 tablespoon whole black peppercorns

1 teaspoon whole cloves

2 cinnamon sticks, preferably Mexican *canela* (see Note, page 21)

½ cup raisins

½ cup prunes

½ cup dried apricots

1 750-ml bottle dry red wine, such as Merlot

½ cup toasted almonds

2 quarts Chicken Broth (page 227)

2 tablespoons salt

Vegetable oil for frying

2 ripe black (sweet) plantains, peeled (see Note, page 153)

3 corn tortillas

2 ounces unsweetened Mexican or bittersweet chocolate, chopped (see Note, page 201)

4 large skinless, boneless chicken breasts, split

1 tablespoon freshly ground black pepper

¼ cup lard (page 224)

White rice, for serving

Bring 2 quarts of water to a boil. In a dry cast-iron skillet, toast the *guajillo*, *pasilla*, and *ancho* chiles over medium-low heat in batches for 2 minutes, until fragrant; turn them and shake the pan so they don't scorch. Put the toasted chiles in a large bowl, cover with the boiling water, and let soak until softened and reconstituted, about 30 minutes.

Return the skillet to a medium-high flame and let it get nice and hot, a good 2 minutes. Rub the onion, garlic, tomatoes, and tomatillos with the olive oil. Lay the vegetables in the hot pan and roast, turning occasionally, until soft and well charred on all sides, about 10 minutes. Put the vegetables in a bowl to let them cool a bit.

In a small dry skillet, toast the cumin, fennel, peppercorns, cloves, and cinnamon for 2 minutes, shaking the pan so they don't scorch. Put the spices in a clean coffee grinder or spice mill, grind to a powder, and set aside.

In a medium saucepan, combine the raisins, prunes, and apricots. Place over medium-low heat and pour in the wine. Simmer to reconstitute the fruit and to evaporate the wine down to a syrup, about 30 minutes, stirring occasionally.

Put the chiles, along with their soaking water, in a blender and purée until completely smooth (you will have to do this in batches). Add the chile purée to a large, heavy pot as you work.

Put the rest of the mole components together in a blender—the charred vegetables, the ground spices, the reconstituted fruit, and the almonds. Again, purée in batches until completely smooth. Add this purée to the large pot of chiles. Put the pot over medium heat, pour in the broth, and add 1 tablespoon of the salt. Simmer for about 1 hour, stirring occasionally, until thick.

Meanwhile, in a deep skillet, heat 3 inches of oil to 375°F. (Check the temperature with an instant-read thermometer or sprinkle some *masa* in the hot oil; if it sizzles, the oil is ready.) Slice the plantains into 1-inch-thick slices and fry, a few at a time, carefully rotating them so they brown evenly, about 3 minutes. Set aside on paper towels to drain.

Char the corn tortillas directly on an electric or gas stove just until they begin to blacken and smoke.

Add the fried plantains, the chocolate, and the charred tortillas to the sauce; stir all the ingredients together. Remove from the heat, ladle into a blender, and purée again.

Season the chicken breasts on both sides with the remaining tablespoon of salt and the pepper. In a large, deep skillet or Dutch oven, melt the lard over medium-high heat. When the lard is smoking and rippling, add the chicken and brown each side for 4 minutes. Pour the mole over the chicken to cover and simmer over moderate heat for 20 minutes, until no longer pink. Serve over white rice.

{the restaurant:
    salads and entrées}

LAS VERDURAS
{the salads}

ENSALADA DE BACALAO
{salt cod salad}

ENSALADA DE NOPALES Y CAMARONES
{cactus salad with shrimp}

CÓCTEL DE PULPO
{octopus cocktail}

ENSALADA DE PALMITO
{hearts of palm salad}

ENSALADA DEL MERCADO
{market salad}

LOS PLATOS PRINCIPALES
{the entrées}

HÍGADO ESTILO CHINO-LATINO
{liver chinese-latin style}

CHILES EN NOGADA
{stuffed poblanos with walnut sauce}

ARROZ CON POLLO
{chicken with rice}

POLLO BORRACHO
{drunken chicken}

ASOPAO DE MARISCOS
{puerto rican soupy rice with seafood}

PESCADO CON MOJO DE AJO
{fish with garlic-butter sauce}

ENCHILADO DE CAMARÓNES
{shrimp in spicy tomato-and-pepper sauce}

PESCADO EN SALSA DE COCO
{fish in coconut broth}

ESCABECHE DE PESCADO
{pickled cooked fish}

PASTELÓN DE PLÁTANOS CON CARNE
{puerto rican meat-and-plantain pie}

THROUGHOUT THE WEEK, Latin Americans don't dine

out much—they may grab a taco for lunch or sit at a *fonda*-type counter for a soup, but you won't see a lot of full-service tables packed on a Tuesday night. Grabbing a quick bite to eat is an everyday occurrence, but truly dining out—with family and friends in a restaurant, with a menu and a waiter—is not. You don't go out to dinner for sustenance; you have dinner at home, with your family. Part of the reason is economic—dining out costs more. But a larger reason is just plain cultural: A meal is really about family and intimacy, and you get these at home. Even if you're short on time, it's much more common to get something to go than to go out.

Saturday and Sunday nights are different. Then, Latins dine out, often with the whole family, at a *comedor*—a real full-service restaurant in the American sense. This chapter is about the "fancy" food that you get in a *comedor,* at a sit-down meal, with a full menu, from appetizers to drinks and dessert. Just as the structure of the meal is more complex, the dishes themselves are more elaborate. Alcohol is served—not only beer, but mixed drinks if you want. There's a bartender, a waiter, the whole bit, not just a counter or self-serve.

The concept of eating out only on the weekend may seem foreign to many Americans—and most New Yorkers—who take it as a given that there is a wealth of sit-down restaurants, of varying cuisines and prices, and you're free to visit one on any given night of the week. I even know some people who eat out *every* night of the week. This is not a part of the Latin mind-set: If you're seated at a restaurant with a cloth napkin, sipping a fresh margarita, it's Saturday or Sunday. And the recipes in this chapter are what you're eating.

PRE-HISPANIC CUISINE

Before the Spaniards arrived in what then became known as the New World, the diet in this hemisphere was very different. It included grains and legumes such as corn, quinoa, and beans; wild game birds as well as iguanas and rabbit; indigenous fruits and vegetables such as sour oranges and melons; peppers and their smoked-and-dried counterparts, chiles; even beetles and grasshoppers. The Spanish brought a culinary revolution: horses to work the land; cattle and pigs for protein; olive oil and capers from Europe; and spices from Asia. So the Latin American cuisine we know today isn't based purely on European imports, nor purely on indigenous products—it's *mestizo,* a mixture. And the same can be said of so many things in Latin America: They are *mestizo.*

ENSALADA DE **BACALAO**

{salt cod salad}

Different cultures use different types of fish depending on what's available, and cod is often the most popular and expensive, particularly if it's boneless. Local markets may sell dried haddock or pollock, which make modest substitutes. Cod is sold in pieces, while haddock and pollock are generally sold whole.

This dish originated in Puerto Rico—its version of a seafood appetizer or light lunch, in the same vein as ceviche or shrimp cocktail. I am a fan of preparing and serving *bacalao* cold as opposed to cooking it and serving hot; the flavor is fresh and vibrant. I like to cook bacalao in milk because I believe it pulls out any additional salt that has remained after soaking the fish.

SERVES 4 TO 6

2 pounds dried salted boneless salt cod (see Note)
1 cup whole milk
1 large red onion, thinly sliced
2 to 3 scallions, white and green parts, finely chopped
¼ cup chopped cilantro
1 avocado, pitted, peeled, and sliced
½ cup halved cherry tomatoes
½ cup extra-virgin olive oil
¼ cup red wine vinegar
   Juice of 1 lime
2 garlic cloves, minced
   Salt and freshly ground black pepper to taste

Soak the *bacalao* in cold water for 24 hours, changing the water three times to remove the majority of the salt. Drain and rinse under cold water and put it in a large pot. Add the milk and enough water to cover by 1 inch. Cook, uncovered, over medium heat for 45 minutes. Drain and set aside to cool. When cool enough to handle, shred the fish into a bowl; take care to get out all the little bones. Add the onion, scallions, cilantro, avocado, and tomatoes.

Whisk together the oil, vinegar, lime juice, garlic, and salt and pepper in a medium bowl. Add the dressing to the salad, toss, and serve.

BACALAO (DRIED SALT COD)

Cod that has been preserved in salt, which removes the moisture, making the fish firm and chewy. *Bacalao* is very popular in Brazil, Italy, Portugal, and Spain, although the cod itself generally comes from Norway. Dried and salted cod has been consumed for over five hundred years. In the fifteenth century, on the Spanish coast, cod began to be salted and dried on rocks to preserve it. In the times of colonial expansion, the long voyages required food-preservation techniques. The drying-and-salting method, besides guaranteeing perfect conservation, maintained all the cod's nutrients and flavor.

Bacalao must be soaked for at least a day in several changes of water before using.

MURAL BY CHICO

ENSALADA DE **NOPALES** Y **CAMARONES**

{cactus salad with shrimp}

In Mexico, the nopal becomes especially important table fare during Lent, when the Catholic Church frowns upon the consumption of meat. A common sight in Mexican markets is the nopal vendor, busy scraping the spines and dicing the pads, which are then ready for the shopper to take home and cook. In a typical Mexican kitchen, *nopales* are boiled and then rinsed to wash away the *babas*, the slimy liquid that exudes during cooking (like okra). I've discovered that grilling the cactus not only adds a world of flavor but also reduces the stickiness. This salad is like a crunchy-tart salsa. It's very simple to make and can be dressed up with shrimp, or served like a taco in a lettuce leaf or in a corn tortilla.

SERVES 4

3 ripe tomatoes, chopped

1/2 medium red onion, diced

1 jalapeño, diced

1/4 cup chopped cilantro

1 garlic clove, minced

1 cup extra-virgin olive oil

4 medium-size fresh *nopales* (cactus pads, see Note)
 Salt and freshly ground black pepper

8 medium shrimp (about 1/2 pound), peeled and deveined with tails on

1/4 cup white wine vinegar
 Lettuce leaves or corn tortillas, for serving

In a large bowl, mix the tomatoes, onion, jalapeño, and cilantro. Set aside.

Preheat a ridged grill pan over a medium-high flame. Combine the garlic and 1/2 cup of the oil in a mixing bowl. Dip the *nopales* in the garlic oil to coat; season both sides with salt and pepper to taste. Place the cactus on the hot grill and cook until limp, about 4 minutes on each side. Cool, cut the pads into 1/4-inch-thick strips, and add to the salad.

Dip the shrimp in the remaining garlic oil to coat and season. Grill for 3 minutes on each side, until firm and pink; add them to the bowl. Pour in the vinegar and remaining 1/2 cup of oil, toss to coat, and season with salt and pepper to taste. Serve in a lettuce leaf or corn tortilla.

NOPALES

The fleshy, oval paddles from the prickly pear cactus; the fruit is called tuna. *Nopales* add an unusual but great texture to dishes, with a flavor like a tart green bean. Very common in Mexico, this vegetable gained popularity outside of the Mexican culture due to its numerous nutritional and health benefits: It is high in fiber and vitamins A, C, and B complex. Look for medium-small, firm, and green pads. If fresh *nopales* are not available, substitute the jarred variety, although there is no comparing the flavor. The jarred are cut in thin strips and preserved in brine; be sure to drain and rinse before using.

To prepare fresh *nopales*, cut off the ends of the paddle. Shave off the needles on both sides of the cactus with a paring knife or vegetable peeler. Rinse under cold water.

CÓCTEL DE **PULPO**

This ceviche-ish seafood cocktail is typically seen alongside other chilled seafood cocktails at Sandy's on 116th Street and Second Avenue. When purchasing octopus, select the smaller and younger variety, which are the most tender. Plus, beating it with a meat mallet further breaks down the flesh, so it has a nice chew without being rubbery. Make sure the octopus has no odor or slime, and rinse before cooking. I don't use the body of the octopus, only the legs. Some superstitious cooks believe that tossing a wine cork in the cooking liquid gives the octopus good vibes and adds to one's virility. Serving this in lettuce cups makes for an edible "bowl" and a great presentation. The paprika vinaigrette is Spanish inspired, and is also great drizzled on roasted potatoes or with grilled seafood.

SERVES 8

1 whole octopus (2 to 4 pounds)
1 large white onion, unpeeled and halved
1 head of garlic, unpeeled and halved
1 tablespoon dried Mexican oregano (see Note, page 73)
3 bay leaves
1 teaspoon whole black peppercorns
1 lemon, halved
1 cup dry white wine, such as sauvignon blanc
½ red onion, thinly sliced
1 red bell pepper, cored and thinly sliced
6 cherry tomatoes, halved
½ cup coarsely chopped cilantro
8 large romaine hearts

PAPRIKA VINAIGRETTE

1 teaspoon Spanish paprika
1 garlic clove, minced
Juice of 2 limes
½ cup extra-virgin olive oil
1 teaspoon salt
½ teaspoon freshly ground black pepper

Rinse the octopus thoroughly under cold water and pat dry with paper towels. Lay the octopus out on a flat surface. Using a smooth meat mallet or rolling pin, pound the tentacles to tenderize the meat. Put the whole octopus in a large pot with the white onion, garlic, oregano, bay leaves, and peppercorns. Squeeze in the lemon juice, and then toss the halves in there too. Pour in the wine (the cork is optional) and 2 quarts of cold water. Place over a medium-high flame and bring to a boil; reduce the heat to medium-low, cover, and simmer for 30 minutes. Shut off the heat and let the octopus soak in the broth for another 20 minutes to gently finish cooking.

Remove the octopus to a cutting board and let cool. Using a sharp knife, cut the tentacles from the body. Slice the tentacles very thin, about ¼ inch thick, and put in a large bowl; discard the body. Add the red onion, red pepper, tomatoes, and cilantro. Toss to combine.

To make the vinaigrette, combine the paprika, garlic, lime juice, and oil in a small bowl. Season with the salt and pepper and whisk. Pour the vinaigrette over the octopus salad and toss well to coat. Cover and chill for 30 minutes to let the flavors marry.

To serve, spoon the salad into the lettuce cups and fold it up like a taco to eat.

ENSALADA DE **PALMITO**

{hearts of palm salad}

Hearts of palm is the national ingredient in Dominican eateries; it is used in both hot and cold dishes. If you travel around tropical Latin America, you will see hearts of palm used again and again in places like Veracruz, Central America, Brazil, and Costa Rica. My favorite use of this delicate vegetable is in salad, where the light, crisp taste of the hearts of palm has a starring role. Canned hearts of palm are widely available, while fresh are difficult to get, plus extremely perishable.

SERVES 4

- 1 14-ounce can hearts of palm, drained, rinsed, and thinly sliced (see Note)
- 1 red bell pepper, cored and thinly sliced
- 1 yellow bell pepper, cored and thinly sliced
- 1 jalapeño, thinly sliced
- ½ medium red onion, thinly sliced
- 1 garlic clove, slivered
- 2 tablespoons chopped cilantro
- Juice of 1 lime
- ¼ cup extra-virgin olive oil
- 1 teaspoon salt
- ½ teaspoon freshly ground black pepper
- ½ medium pineapple

In a large bowl, combine the hearts of palm with the peppers, jalapeño, red onion, garlic, and cilantro. Toss to mix. Add the lime juice, oil, salt, and pepper. Toss again so the vegetables are well coated.

Scoop out the flesh of the pineapple with a melon baller or serving spoon; try to keep the pineapple in big pieces and leave the shell intact. Slice the pineapple chunks in thin strips and add it to the salad. Toss everything together and serve inside the hollowed-out pineapple.

HEARTS OF PALM

Literally just that: the inner portion of the stem of palm trees. The ivory-colored cylinders are firm and smooth and the flavor is reminiscent of an artichoke heart. Widely available canned, they should be rinsed before using. Brazil is the biggest producer of hearts of palm, while the Dominican Republic remains the largest consumer.

ENSALADA DEL **MERCADO**

Variations of this refreshing summer salad are sold from street carts in plastic bags. On Twenty-fourth and Valencia in San Francisco's Mission District, a lady sits on the corner and sells this for just a dollar. The mango and jicama are put into a plastic bag; lime, salt, and pepper are added; and the vendor shakes the bag to mix. The salad is eaten with toothpicks as you walk. As in most Mexican salads, lettuce is not used as a main ingredient. This fresh and rustic salad is a real palate cleanser. Mango, chile, and lime are the sweet, spicy, and tart triple threat that is seen over and over again in Mexican cuisine; the creamy avocado is my own special touch.

SERVES 4

1 chile de árbol, stemmed and seeded (see Note, page 231)
2 small cucumbers, peeled and seeded
½ pound jicama, peeled
1 mango, peeled and cut into chunks
Juice of 2 limes
Salt and freshly ground black pepper
1 avocado, pitted, peeled, and sliced
¼ cup extra-virgin olive oil

In a dry cast-iron skillet, toast the chile over medium-low heat for 2 minutes, until fragrant; turn it and shake the pan so it doesn't scorch. Put the toasted chile in a clean coffee grinder or spice mill and grind to a powder.

Cut the cucumbers and jicama into 2-inch-long, ⅛-inch-thick matchsticks and add to a mixing bowl with the mango and lime juice. Toss to combine and season with salt and pepper to taste. Pile the mixture onto serving plates and drizzle with the juices in the bottom of the bowl. Fan the avocado slices on top of the salad and sprinkle with a fair amount of the chile powder. Drizzle with the oil and serve.

HÍGADO ESTILO CHINO-LATINO

{liver chinese-latin style}

This is a spin-off of a dish that my mother has on the menu at her restaurant, Zarela. It reminds me of when I was younger, working at Mom's place, and I learned how to butcher liver. At first I was squeamish, but after I prepared the liver and tasted how good it was, all my fears were quickly reduced—very much like the chicken broth in this recipe. This dish reflects the important contributions that Chinese ingredients have made to Latin cooking. My exposure to Cuban cooking has shown me that soy sauce is a vital crossover ingredient, which is why I added it to this rendition of my mom's dish.

SERVES 4

- 1   cup all-purpose flour
- 1   tablespoon salt
- 1   tablespoon freshly ground black pepper
- 1   pound beef liver, cut into ¼-inch slices
- 1   tablespoon extra-virgin olive oil
- ½   cup diced smoked bacon
- ½   large white onion, thinly sliced
- 2   garlic cloves, slivered
- 1   pickled jalapeño, sliced (see Note)
- 2   tablespoons soy sauce
- 1   cup Chicken Broth (page 227)
     Juice of 1 lemon
- 2   tablespoons (¼ stick) unsalted butter
- 1   tablespoon chopped cilantro

Pour the flour in a shallow dish and season with the salt and pepper. Dredge the liver in the seasoned flour. In large skillet, heat the oil over a medium flame. When the oil begins to smoke, add the liver in batches, making sure not to crowd the pan. Cook on each side for 3 minutes, until golden brown. Remove the browned liver to a platter and keep warm.

In the same pan, add the bacon to the liver drippings and cook over medium heat for 5 minutes, until crispy. Add the onion, garlic, and jalapeño and cook, stirring, for 5 minutes. Add the soy sauce and chicken broth and let the liquid cook down until reduced by half, about 5 minutes. Add the lemon juice and butter. When the butter has melted, add the cilantro and season with salt and pepper to taste. Pour the sauce over the liver and serve.

PICKLED JALAPEÑOS

Usually come in cans packed with onions and carrots; all are deliciously spicy and edible. Jalapeños are named after the famous chile originating from Jalapa, Veracruz, which is able to travel all over the world through pickling or brining. Pickled jalapeños are a favorite condiment at taco stands all over the United States and Mexico.

CHILES EN **NOGADA**

{stuffed poblanos with walnut sauce}

This dish originated in the Mexican city of Puebla with the colonial nuns. It is always associated with September, *el mes de la patria*, because it features the red, white, and green colors of the Mexican flag—the green of the pepper, the white of the sauce, and the red of the pomegranate seeds. Because it looks as good as it tastes, it is considered somewhat of a show-off dish, served at weddings and the like, and is more special than the standard Mexican chiles rellenos. The following recipe is an authentic, uncomplicated version of the Puebla classic, originally taught to me by my grandmother. It was also featured in the film *Like Water for Chocolate* because of its seductive allure.

SERVES 6

SAUCE

- 1½ cups toasted and coarsely chopped walnuts
- ¼ cup coarsely chopped cilantro
- 1 8-ounce package cream cheese, at room temperature
- 1 cup half-and-half
- 1 tablespoon sugar
- Salt and freshly ground black pepper

FILLING

- 3 tablespoons vegetable oil, plus more for frying
- ½ pound ground beef
- ½ pound ground pork
- 1 medium white onion, diced
- 2 garlic cloves, minced
- 1 15-ounce can chopped tomatoes
- 1 teaspoon ground cinnamon, preferably Mexican *canela* (see Note, page 21)
- ½ teaspoon ground cumin
- ½ teaspoon ground cloves
- Salt and freshly ground black pepper

1 Granny Smith apple, unpeeled and cut into ½-inch cubes
¼ cup raisins soaked in 1 cup tequila
¼ cup toasted slivered almonds
½ cup sliced pimiento-stuffed green olives
6 large *poblano* peppers (see Note, page 85)
1 cup pomegranate seeds, for garnish

To make the sauce, put the walnuts, cilantro, cream cheese, half-and-half, and sugar in a food processor. Pulse to combine the ingredients, then purée until the mixture is the consistency of mayonnaise. Season with salt and pepper to taste. Cover and reserve, but do not refrigerate.

To make the filling, heat 3 tablespoons of the oil over a medium flame in a large, deep skillet or Dutch oven. When the oil begins to smoke, add the ground beef and pork, stirring and pressing with the back of a wooden spoon to break up any clumps. Cook until the meat is thoroughly browned, about 10 minutes. Add the onion and garlic and sauté for 3 minutes. Add the tomatoes, cinnamon, cumin, and cloves, and season with salt and pepper to taste. Fold in the apple, raisins, almonds, and olives. Give everything a good stir and cover. Lower the heat to keep it warm.

Heat ½ inch of oil in a large, heavy skillet and place over a medium-high flame. When the oil begins to smoke, fry the *poblanos*, 3 at a time, turning once or twice so they are blistered on all sides. As they are done, remove them from the pan and drain briefly on paper towels. Put the peppers in a bowl, cover with plastic wrap, and let them sweat for about 5 minutes to loosen the skins. Gently rub off as much of the charred skin as possible, but do not rinse with water. Cut a slit lengthwise along the side of each pepper, keeping the stem and tip intact. Carefully pull out the seeds and inner membranes through the opening, being sure not to tear the pepper.

Carefully spoon the filling into the poblanos until it feels full, not bursting. Pool the walnut sauce on the base of a platter, arrange the stuffed chiles on top, and garnish with pomegranate seeds. The dish may be served warm or at room temperature.

ARROZ CON POLLO

Every part of Latin America claims to have given birth to the famous chicken-and-rice dish called arroz con pollo. In fact, there are as many recipes as there are cooks. This is an easy dish to prepare, making it a favorite for Sunday lunches; it is kind of like the Latino jambalaya. I learned a great family trick of standing a wooden spoon up in the arroz con pollo to check the rice-to-broth ratio; if the spoon stands up, it's perfect. This illustrates how Latins feel the soul of the food, without measuring.

SERVES 8

- 5 garlic cloves, 3 smashed, 2 minced
- 2 tablespoons plus ¼ cup coarsely chopped fresh *recao* (see Note)
- 1 tablespoon cumin seeds
- 1 tablespoon coriander seeds
- 1 teaspoon cayenne
- 2 teaspoons salt
- 1 teaspoon freshly ground black pepper
- 2 tablespoons orange juice
- 3 tablespoons extra-virgin olive oil
- 1 whole frying chicken (about 3½ pounds), cut into 8 serving pieces
- ½ pound Spanish chorizo sausage (about 2 links), diced (see Note, page 19)
- ½ pound cured ham, diced
- 1 medium white onion, diced
- 1 red bell pepper, cored and chopped
- 1 *cubanella* or green bell pepper, cored and chopped (see Note, page 43)
- 2 bay leaves
- 2 teaspoons *bijol* or saffron (see Note)
- 2 cups long-grain white rice
- 1 15-ounce can chopped tomatoes
- 3 cups Chicken Broth (page 227)
- 1 cup pimiento-stuffed green olives
- 2 tablespoons capers, drained

Using a mortar and pestle, mash the 3 smashed garlic cloves, 2 tablespoons of the *recao*, the cumin, coriander, cayenne, salt, and pepper. Drizzle the spice mix with the orange juice and 2 tablespoons of the oil to moisten it, and continue to mash everything together to create a smooth paste. Rinse the chicken pieces and pat them dry. Rub the chicken with the spice paste and let it marinate for 2 hours to develop the flavor.

Place a large, wide Dutch oven over medium heat and coat with the remaining 1 tablespoon of oil. Add the chorizo and ham and cook for 5 minutes, until the sausage gets crispy; remove with a slotted spoon and drain on paper towels. Add the chicken pieces, skin-side down; you may have to work in batches. Brown the chicken for 6 minutes on each side and then remove it to a platter.

Preheat the oven to 350°F.

To make the *sofrito*, add the onion, 2 minced garlic cloves, peppers, bay leaves, and *bijol* to the pan. Cook and stir for 10 minutes over medium heat, until the vegetables have softened; don't let them brown. Fold in the rice so the grains are well coated in the *sofrito*. Nestle the chicken pieces, chorizo, and ham back into the pan. Pour in the tomatoes and broth, and season with salt and pepper to taste. Scatter the olives and capers on top. Bring to a boil, cover, and bake for 40 to 45 minutes, or until the chicken is done and the rice is tender and has absorbed most of the liquid. Shower with the remaining chopped *recao* before serving.

BIJOL

Like turmeric or saffron, a yellow spice used mainly as a coloring agent. Annato has a similar use, and neither have much flavor.

RECAO

Also known as *culantro* and sawleaf herb, because of the jagged edges of the leaves. In fact, they look like long quills. The herb is sold fresh, in bunches, and is used as a main staple in Puerto Rican cooking and sofritos. Although less pungent than *recao*, cilantro works fine as a substitute.

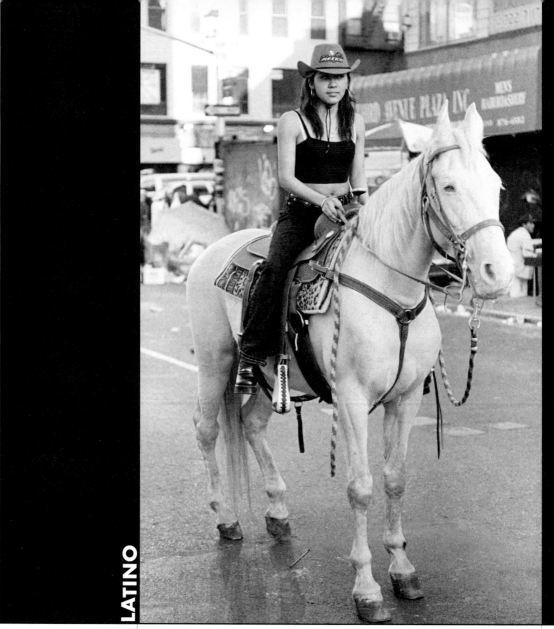

EL TOMATE LATINO

You may think that the tomato is Italy's gift to the world. While it's true that Italians have done wonderful things with the tomato, it didn't originate there—in fact, tomatoes didn't arrive in Europe until Spaniards brought them back from Peru in the sixteenth century. They then traveled to the Spanish kingdom of Naples, and soon throughout Italy and the rest of the Mediterranean. So of course tomato sauce isn't an Italian invention either: Think about the classic sauce *pico de gallo,* or any of the puréed salsas—all Latin, all popular before a pasta was ever red-sauced.

POLLO **BORRACHO**

{drunken chicken}

My mom has a version of this on her menu at Zarela. The beauty of this dish is that you can throw everything in the pot and walk away. The result is deep flavor and a smell to die for. Tequila is acidic and tenderizes the meat, creating a moist chicken. It's an easy preparation and the ingredients are very accessible.

SERVES 4 TO 8

1 whole frying chicken (about 3 1/2 pounds), cut into 8 serving pieces
1 tablespoon dried Mexican oregano (see Note, page 73)
1 tablespoon salt
1 1/2 teaspoons freshly ground black pepper
1/4 cup extra-virgin olive oil
1 large white onion, thickly sliced
3 garlic cloves
1 bay leaf
1/2 cup dry white wine, such as sauvignon blanc
1/2 cup tequila
1 cup pimiento-stuffed green olives

Rinse the chicken pieces and pat them dry; season with the oregano, salt, and pepper.

Coat a large Dutch oven or ovenproof skillet with the oil and place over medium-high heat. When the oil just begins to smoke, add the chicken pieces, skin-side down; you may have to work in batches. Brown the chicken for 6 minutes on each side and then remove it to a platter.

Preheat the oven to 375°F.

Reduce the flame to medium-low. Add the onion, garlic, and bay leaf to the pan drippings and sauté until the onion is soft, about 5 minutes. Pour in the wine and tequila. Nestle the chicken back in the pot and scatter the olives on top. Cover and roast in the oven for 30 minutes, or until cooked through. Season with salt and pepper to taste and serve.

ASOPAO DE **MARISCOS**

{puerto rican soupy rice with seafood}

Puerto Rico's beloved rice-based stew is a cross between soupy risotto and paella. In Puerto Rican eateries in the United States, *asopao* is served as a Saturday special. The variations are countless, and you can add almost any type of meat. I use shrimp and crab here, but you'll also find it made with either chicken or pigeon peas.

SERVES 6 TO 8

½ cup *achiote* oil (page 225)

¼ pound cured ham, diced

1 medium white onion, chopped

2 garlic cloves, minced

1 red bell pepper, cored and chopped

1 cup dry white wine, such as sauvignon blanc

1 15-ounce can tomato purée

2 tablespoons capers, drained

1 tablespoon chopped fresh oregano

1 teaspoon salt

½ teaspoon freshly ground black pepper

1½ cups long-grain rice

5 cups Shrimp Stock (page 229)

16 medium shrimp (about 1 pound), peeled and deveined with tails on

1 pound lump crabmeat, preferably Dungeness, picked over for shells

1 cup frozen or fresh sweet green peas (see Note, page 25)

1 jarred pimiento, cut in strips

1 lime, quartered

Coat a large pot or Dutch oven with 3 tablespoons of the oil over medium heat. Add the ham and cook for 5 minutes to caramelize. Add the onion, garlic, and pepper and cook, stirring, for 10 minutes, until the vegetables have softened; don't let them brown. Pour in the wine and continue to cook until the liquid is evaporated. Add the tomatoes, capers, oregano, salt, and pepper, and cook for 5 minutes to mingle the flavors. Fold in the rice and cook for 1 minute to coat. Pour in the broth, cover, reduce the heat to low, and simmer for 20 minutes.

Fold in the shrimp, crab, and peas. Cook for 5 minutes, until the shrimp is firm and the rice is tender but still soupy. Serve in wide bowls, garnished with a few slices of pimiento, a tablespoon drizzle of the oil, and a squeeze of lime.

PESCADO CON MOJO DE AJO

{fish with garlic-butter sauce}

Mojo de ajo is a traditional Spanish pan sauce brought to the New World by the settlers in Mexico. Made with garlic, citrus, and herbs, it's light and great for most seafood—and one of the few ways you can order fish in Latin places. Langostinos and shrimp are great with this also. Serve with white or yellow rice (page 158).

SERVES 4

1 cup all-purpose flour

1 tablespoon salt

1 tablespoon freshly ground black pepper

4 flounder or sole fillets (6 to 8 ounces each)

¼ cup extra-virgin olive oil

4 garlic cloves, slivered

8 cherry tomatoes, halved

2 pickled jalapeños, sliced

Juice of 1 lemon

2 cups Shrimp Stock (page 229)

1 tablespoon unsalted butter

2 tablespoons chopped cilantro

Preheat the oven to 450°F.

Combine the flour, salt, and pepper in a dish, and dredge the fish. Heat 2 tablespoons of the oil in a large nonstick skillet over a medium-high flame. When the oil begins to smoke, add the fillets and cook for 3 minutes. Flip the fish over and transfer the pan to the oven. Bake for 5 minutes, until the fish is flaky. Remove the fillets to a paper towel–lined plate and keep warm.

Return the skillet to the stovetop over medium heat and add the remaining 2 tablespoons of oil. Add the garlic and cook, stirring, for 2 minutes, until golden but not burned. Add the tomatoes, jalapeños, lemon juice, and stock. Cook for 5 minutes to reduce down to about 1 cup. (See variation below.) Stir in the butter to thicken and emulsify the sauce. Toss in the chopped cilantro and season with salt and pepper to taste. Drizzle the sauce over the fish and serve.

VARIATION: ALCAPARRADA

To make *acaparrada*, a Spanish-influenced sauce, purée the following ingredients in a blender: ¼ cup pitted green olives, such as *manzanilla*; 2 tablespoons capers, drained; and 1 roasted red bell pepper, peeled and seeded. Add this purée after the sauce reduces but before the butter.

ENCHILADO DE **CAMARONES**

{shrimp in spicy tomato-ard-pepper sauce}

Lobster, scallops, and other types of shellfish are often used in this classic Cuban specialty because they're abundant off the coast of Miami, where the dish is hugely popular. Serve with Pigeon Pea Rice (page 160).

SERVES 4

¼	cup extra-virgin olive oil
1	medium white onion, diced
2	garlic cloves, minced
1	red bell pepper, cored and diced
1	green bell pepper, cored and diced
1	*cubanella* or green bell pepper, cored and diced (see Note, page 43)
1	canned *chipotle* in adobo, chopped
6	*ajícito* chiles, diced (see Note)
2	bay leaves
1	ripe tomato, chopped
	Salt and freshly ground black pepper
1	cup dry sherry
1	15-ounce can tomato purée
1	quart Shrimp Stock (page 229)
16	medium shrimp (about 1 pound), peeled and deveined with tails on
½	cup chopped cilantro
1	lemon, cut in wedges, for serving

Coat a large Dutch oven with the oil and place over medium heat. When the oil begins to smoke, add the onion, garlic, peppers, chiles, and bay leaves. Cook and stir for 15 minutes, until the vegetables have softened; don't let them brown. Add the chopped tomato and stir until soft; season with salt and pepper to taste. Add in the sherry and cook for 5 minutes. Add the tomato purée and shrimp stock; bring up to a simmer. Drop in the shrimp and poach for 5 minutes, until cooked through. Shower with cilantro and serve with lemon wedges.

AJÍCITO CHILE

Also called *cacucha*. This fresh chile does not have a dried counterpart. *Ajícitos* have the sweetness of the habanero without the intense heat.

PESCADO EN SALSA DE COCO

{fish in coconut broth}

Coconut adds a Caribbean flavor to this dish from the Dominican Republic and Cuba. A favorite on island menus, the fish and coconut combo is also very popular in Brazil, where both are plentiful. This delicate and delicious dish is served with rice and plantains.

SERVES 4

- 4 red snapper fillets (6 to 8 ounces each)
  Juice of 2 limes
- 2 garlic cloves, minced
- ¼ cup extra-virgin olive oil
- 1 medium white onion, diced
- 1 celery stalk, diced
- 1 serrano, minced
- 1 ripe tomato, chopped
- ½ cup dry white wine, such as sauvignon blanc
- 1 cup Shrimp Stock (page 229)
- 1 14-ounce can unsweetened coconut milk
  Salt and freshly ground black pepper
- ½ cup coarsely chopped mint
- ½ cup toasted shredded coconut

Rinse the snapper and pat dry with paper towels. In a small bowl, mix the lime juice and half of the garlic together; rub it on both sides of the fish and let it sit for 15 minutes.

Heat 2 tablespoons of the oil in a large saucepan over a medium flame. When the oil is hot, add the onion, celery, serrano, and remaining garlic to the pan. Cook, stirring, for 5 minutes, until the vegetables are soft. Add the tomato and wine, and continue to cook for another 5 minutes, to break down the tomatoes and evaporate the liquid. Pour in the stock and coconut milk, season with salt and pepper to taste, and simmer for 15 minutes, until thick enough to coat the back of a spoon.

Meanwhile, heat the remaining 2 tablespoons of oil in a nonstick skillet over a medium-high flame. Scrape off the garlic from the snapper so it won't burn and season both sides with 1 teaspoon each of salt and pepper. When the oil begins to smoke, lay the fillets in the pan. Gently press the fish with a spatula to brown, about 5 minutes. Carefully transfer the fish to the coconut-broth mixture, browned-side up. Toss in the mint, cover, reduce the heat to low, and simmer for 5 minutes to finish cooking the fish all the way through.

Serve the snapper with a ladleful of sauce and garnish with the toasted coconut.

ESCABECHE DE **PESCADO**

{pickled cooked fish}

Escabeche dishes, which use a Spanish technique to preserve cooked fish and poultry, can be widely found throughout Latin America, especially in coastal areas in Mexico, such as Veracruz and Tabasco, where seafood is abundant. Even though *escabeche* is a time-honored preparation, it's a light dish that fits into today's healthy lifestyle. The variations are endless, with different herbs and vegetables. I include jicama, pineapple, capers, and olives to add complexity.

SERVES 4

- 1 cup red wine vinegar
- 1 tablespoon honey
- 1 canned *chipotle* in adobo, finely chopped (see Note, page 71)
- 2 cups Shrimp Stock (page 229)
- 2 tablespoons tomato paste
- ¼ cup extra-virgin olive oil
- 1 red bell pepper, cored and thinly sliced
- 1 yellow bell pepper, cored and thinly sliced
- 1 green bell pepper, cored and thinly sliced
- 1 red onion, thinly sliced
- 1 teaspoon salt
- ½ teaspoon freshly ground black pepper
- 2 tablespoons chopped cilantro
- 2 tablespoons capers, drained
- ½ cup whole green olives, such as manzanilla
- ½ cup chopped jicama
- ¼ cup chopped pineapple
- 4 kingfish or mackerel fillets (6 to 8 ounces each)
- 2 cups mixed greens
- 4 radishes, sliced

In a medium saucepan, combine the vinegar, honey, *chipotle*, stock, and tomato paste. Place over medium heat and simmer for 10 minutes to reduce until thick.

Meanwhile, coat a large skillet with 2 tablespoons of the oil and place over medium heat. When the oil begins to smoke, add the peppers and onion. Cook for 5 minutes, until the vegetables are soft. Scrape the mixture into the pot of broth, stir to incorporate, and season with the salt and pepper. Remove from the heat and fold in the cilantro, capers, olives, jicama, and pineapple. Set aside.

Return the skillet to the stovetop over medium-high heat. Add the remaining 2 tablespoons of oil. When the oil begins to smoke, lay the fish fillets in the pan and cook for 3 minutes on each side. Remove the fillets to a 13 × 9-inch baking dish. Pour the reserved *escabeche* sauce over the fish, cover, and refrigerate for 8 hours or overnight. Serve at room temperature with the mixed greens and sliced radishes.

CENTRAL AMERICA'S CUISINE

The Spanish-speaking countries of Central America—Costa Rica, El Salvador, Honduras, and Nicaragua—aren't hugely diverse in terms of food: Through-out the region, there's a very similar staple diet of rice and beans, with basic proteins of roasted meat, chicken, and fish. What differentiates each country's cuisine are a few well-known national dishes: In Nicaragua, it's a salad known as *vigorón,* made with yuca and cabbage in a citrus dressing; in El Salvador, it's the *pupusa,* a turnover stuffed with beans, meat, or cheese. And throughout the region, tortillas are not common (except in Guatemala, whose cuisine is the most similar to Mexico's)—although corn is the primary grain, it's used as a dough for tamales, *pupusas,* and the like rather than tortillas.

So if you come across a restaurant that announces itself as Nicaraguan, don't expect to find something totally different from the place across the street that serves Salvadoran food. Chances are the menus are nearly identical. But you'll probably find one or two items you haven't seen in tons of other places, and that's what you should order: whatever's unique.

PASTELÓN DE **PLÁTANOS** CON **CARNE**

{puerto rican meat-and-plantain pie}

This popular Puerto Rican casserole, also known as *piñon,* is served during the holidays and as a rotating weekly special. Yellow plantains are layered with meat and cheese, baked, and then cut like a lasagne. And like lasagne, the possibilities for fillings are endless: The versatile *Picadillo* on page 117 is great; also try the *Gorditas* chicken filling (page 89) and the *Chiles en Nogada* filling (page 140). This casserole is ideal for leftovers. Some cooks mash the plantains with flour and butter and spread it in the pan so it is more like a dough, but I like to maintain the integrity of the plantains' shape and texture by keeping them intact.

SERVES 8 TO 12

- 10 yellow plantains, peeled (see Note, page 153)
   Vegetable oil for frying
   Salt
- 4 eggs, separated
- 2 tablespoons (¼ stick) unsalted butter, for greasing the baking dish
- 1 recipe *Picadillo* (page 117)
- 2 cups grated *Manchego* cheese (see Note)
   Crema fresca or sour cream, for garnish

Cut the plantains in half, and then cut each half lengthwise into 2 slices, creating 4 slices of each plantain. Heat 3 inches of oil in a deep skillet to 375°F. (Check the temperature with an instant-read thermometer or sprinkle some flour in the hot oil; if it sizzles, the oil is ready.) Fry the plantains a few at a time, carefully rotating them so they brown evenly, about 3 minutes. Set aside on a platter lined with paper towels to drain. Season with salt to taste.

In a mixing bowl, beat the egg whites until foamy. Add a pinch of salt and whip to stiff, not dry, peaks. In a separate bowl, lightly beat the egg yolks and then fold them gently into the beaten whites.

Preheat the oven to 400°F.

Grease the bottom and sides of a 13 × 9-inch baking dish with the butter. Arrange half of the plantains in a single layer on the bottom and up the sides of the dish. Using a spatula, spread a thin layer of the whipped eggs over the plantains to fill in the cracks. Spread half of the *picadillo* filling evenly over the eggs and sprinkle with half of the cheese. Repeat the layers with the remaining ingredients. Bake for 30 minutes, until the egg is set and the cheese is bubbling. Garnish each serving with a dollop of *crema fresca*.

MANCHEGO

A buttery-yellow sheep's cheese introduced to Mexico from the Spanish region of La Mancha that is popular outside of Mexico as well. It is good for melting or for serving with fruit or crackers. The flavor can be sharp and salty. *Manchego* is widely available north of the border, but sharp Cheddar is a good substitute.

YELLOW AND BLACK PLANTAINS

The more mature, ripened variety of the green plantain. The fruit gets sweeter and less starchy as it ages. Green plantains will ripen to yellow and then black in about a week sitting out on the counter.

To peel yellow or black plantains, cut off the ends and discard. With a paring knife, make 3 shallow slits lengthwise along the seams of the skin and peel away.

{the market: vegetables and side dishes}

ARROZ AMARILLO
{yellow rice}

MOROS Y CRISTIANOS
{cuban black beans and rice}

ARROZ CON GANDULES
{pigeon peas with rice}

HABICHUELAS DOMINICANAS
{dominican-style red beans}

FRÍJOLES BORRACHOS
{drunken beans}

PURÉ DE BONIATO
{mashed boniato}

GUINEOS VERDES CON MOJO
{green bananas with citrus-
garlic sauce}

FRÍJOLES NEGROS REFRITOS
{refried black beans}

FRITURAS DE YUCA
{yuca fritters}

PLÁTANOS RELLENOS
{stuffed plantains}

SOPA SECA DE FIDEOS
{little pasta in roasted
tomato broth}

PAPAS CHORREADAS
{colombian-style potatoes}

CALABACITAS CON PICO DE
GALLO
{sautéed zucchini with fresh
salsa}

ELOTES ASADOS
{roasted corn with chile-lime
butter}

QUELITES
{sautéed greens}

THE CENTRAL MARKET THAT IS part of the core of

Latin life never really took hold in the United States, though it's not entirely absent. New York has two excellent Latin markets: La Marquetta at Park Avenue and 166th Street in Spanish Harlem, just a short subway ride from my home; and the Essex Street Market on the Lower East Side, just a couple of blocks from my restaurant. Both are run by the New York City Economic Development Corporation, and both are run by Alberto Padilla, a true hero to the community for his revitalization of this treasured Latin tradition.

A supermarket culture has never been a part of the Latin food-shopping mind-set. We prefer to buy from individual vendors, whose names and faces and accents we know, instead of from a faceless corporation. We like to move around the market from stall to stall—here for meat, there for vegetables, over there for chiles (even back around the corner for a new T-shirt). Acquiring each ingredient involves a personal interaction. We haggle, we're choosy, we're critical, and we're vocal— and sometimes we get that extra tomato on the house, just because. Shopping for nightly dinner is fun when you go to the same market every afternoon.

The Essex Street Market is my inspiration. For the set menu at Paladar, we buy food from purveyors, with whom we have standing orders and accounts and terms and paperwork. But first thing every day, I go to the Essex Street Market for the daily specials—I walk around, decide what looks good that day, buy it, take it back to the kitchen, and *make* something. The market keeps me in touch with what's really fun about cooking: choosing an ingredient because it's perfect today, and creating a dish to showcase it.

Nearly everybody shopping in the market is Latin, as are the vendors, and so the whole place has an unmistakable air of being in a different land. All our ingredients are here: the wild-looking Latin tubers like *malanga, batata,* yautia, and yuca are piled high; you can buy small slices to order instead of a whole eight-pound *calabaza;* there are plastic bags with a stew-flavored mix of cilantro, garlic, and *ajícito* peppers (which have the flavor of the insanely hot habanero chile, but not the insane heat); the butcher is selling reasonably sized cuts of *cabrito* (young goat) and *masa de puerco* (diced pork shoulder, ready for braising to make *pasteles,* Puerto Rican tamales); and our beloved canned products such as beans and *chiles en adobo* are here, along with dried fish and more.

The Essex Street Market and La Marquetta are not mirror images of the markets in the homeland: They don't have *fondas* where you can eat, nor the breadth and variety of goods. You can still buy clothes, hats, toys, music, and bags as well as your groceries, but you can't get *everything* you'll ever need, as you can in Mexico. There are no artisans here selling hand-loomed textiles or hand-thrown pottery, and this is not a farmer's market filled with *campesinos* who loaded up the burro for a trip into town. This is New York City, after all, and just a few blocks from the heart of SoHo, one of the fanciest neighborhoods on the planet.

The core of the market is the produce, especially the special fruits and vegetables that are not particularly common outside of the barrio. This chapter will show you what to do with the market produce, which as much as anything tastes like home to me.

ARROZ AMARILLO

{yellow rice}

Every Cuban café has yellow rice on the menu; it's eaten all over the Caribbean as a complement to seafood. Because of the saffron, it is sometimes referred to as Spanish rice, and may also include peas and carrots, making it reminiscent of paella. The Latin method of baking rice in the oven provides more even heat than cooking it on a stove-top, so there is no risk of burning the bottom (although some cooks deem the crusty rice stuck to the pot the pinnacle of a perfect Spanish rice). To make classic white rice, omit the coloring agent (*bijol*, saffron, *achiote*) and follow the recipe as directed.

SERVES 4 TO 6

2 tablespoons extra-virgin olive oil
1 medium white onion, diced
1 garlic clove, minced
1 tablespoon *bijol* or saffron, or 1 teaspoon *achiote* paste (see Notes, pages 143 and 225)
2 cups long-grain rice
1 quart Chicken Broth (page 227)
2 teaspoons salt
1 teaspoon freshly ground black pepper

Preheat the oven to 350°F.

Heat the oil in a Dutch oven or other ovenproof pot over a medium flame. Add the onion, garlic, and *bijol*, and cook for 2 minutes, until soft. Fold in the rice and continue to stir until the grains are chalky, about 5 minutes. Add the broth, salt, and pepper. Bring to a boil and give the rice a stir. Cover and bake for 25 minutes. Let the rice stand out of the oven for 5 minutes to finish steaming, and fluff with a fork before serving.

MOROS Y CRISTIANOS

In Latin culture, history shapes everything, including food. The Spanish name translates to "Moors and Christians," which refers to the wars between the dark-skinned Moors (black beans) and the fair-skinned Christian Spaniards (white rice). This dish is different because the beans and rice ultimately are cooked together. Don't make the common mistake of confusing *Moros y Cristianos* with *Congri*, another Cuban rice dish that is made with red beans; substitute red beans for black to make *Congri*.

SERVES 4 TO 6

1 pound dried black turtle beans, picked through and rinsed

2 bay leaves

1 tablespoon dried Mexican oregano (see Note, page 73)

1 tablespoon extra-virgin olive oil

¼ pound bacon, diced

¼ pound cured ham, diced

¼ pound Spanish chorizo sausage (about 1 link), diced (see Note, page 19)

1 medium white onion, diced

2 garlic cloves, chopped

1 red bell pepper, cored and diced

1 green bell pepper, cored and diced

1 teaspoon ground cumin

2 cups long-grain rice

Salt and freshly ground black pepper

Put the beans, bay leaves, and oregano in a large pot, cover with 3 quarts of cold water, and place over medium heat. Cover and cook the beans for 45 minutes (they will only be cooked halfway). Drain the beans and reserve the liquid.

Preheat the oven to 350°F.

Coat a large Dutch oven or other ovenproof pot with the oil and place over medium heat. Add the bacon, ham, and chorizo. Cook for 5 minutes to render the fat from the pork. Add the onion, garlic, and peppers. Cook, stirring, for 5 minutes to soften. Add the cumin, rice, cooked beans, and reserved cooking liquid. Season with salt and pepper to taste, bring to a boil, and give everything a stir. Cover and bake for 25 minutes, until the rice is tender and the liquid is absorbed. Fluff with a fork before serving.

ARROZ CON GANDULES

{pigeon peas with rice}

This dish is traditional for Puerto Rican families on Christmas and other special occasions, such as weddings and communions. Varieties of pork, such as ham, chorizo, and *tocino* (fatback or bacon) are frequently mixed in with the rice. In my opinion, the saltiness and fat overpower the delicate flavor of the pigeon peas. So here is a basic vegetarian version. Serve with the *Enchilado de Camarones* (page 148).

SERVES 4 TO 6

1 pound dried pigeon peas, picked through and rinsed (see Note)

2 bay leaves

¼ cup *achiote* oil (page 225)

1 medium white onion, diced

2 garlic cloves, minced

1 red bell pepper, cored and diced

1 green bell pepper, cored and diced

1 *cubanella* or green bell pepper, cored and diced (see Note, page 43)

1 cup dry white wine, such as sauvignon blanc

1 teaspoon ground cumin

1 teaspoon ground coriander

1 teaspoon cayenne

2 cups long-grain rice

1 tablespoon salt

Put the pigeon peas and bay leaves in a large pot, cover with 2 quarts of cold water, and place over medium heat. Cover and cook the beans until tender, about 1½ hours. Check the water periodically; add more if necessary to keep the peas covered. Drain the pigeon peas and reserve 4 cups of the cooking liquid.

Preheat the oven to 350°F.

Coat a large Dutch oven or other ovenproof pot with the oil and place over medium heat. When the oil begins to smoke, add the onion, garlic, and peppers. Cook, stirring, for 10 minutes, until the vegetables have softened; don't let them brown. Pour in the wine and continue to cook until the liquid is evaporated. Add the cumin, coriander, and cayenne; stir constantly for 5 minutes so the spices don't burn. Pour in the 4 cups of reserved pigeon pea cooking liquid and bring to a boil. Add the rice, reserved pigeon peas, and salt; stir everything together. Cover and bake for 20 to 30 minutes, until the rice is tender and the liquid is absorbed.

PIGEON PEAS

A high-protein legume that is cultivated in India, Africa, and Southeast Asia, but has become a staple of Latin and Caribbean cuisine, and is mostly used in the stews and rice dishes of Cuba, Puerto Rico, and the other Caribbean islands. There, they are regionally called gandules, Congo peas, and tropical peas. In the United States, pigeon peas are particularly popular in the South. In their dried form, they look somewhat similar to green peas, except they are tan with speckles. To add to the confusion, green peas are referred to as gandules also. Pigeon peas have a tough outer skin that even when fully cooked has some texture and resistance when you bite into it. The flavor is buttery and nutty, much like a black-eyed pea. Before serving, taste them to be sure the inside flesh is soft and creamy.

HABICHUELAS **DOMINICANAS**

{dominican-style red beans}

Dominican food is robust and full of flavor, a meld of different ethnic backgrounds such as Spanish, African, and native Indian merges to form this unique cuisine. The history of the Dominican Republic even includes influences from France, as illustrated here by the link to Louisiana—French Creole red beans. The Dominican Republic is the second largest island in the Caribbean and their cuisine often mirrors the larger Cuba. Red beans are a favorite and are typically served with succulent meat, such as *Pernil al Horno* or *Lechón Asado* (pages 118 and 119). The addition of pumpkin makes this dish undeniably Caribbean. Serve with yellow rice (page 158).

SERVES 6 TO 8

- 2 tablespoons lard (page 224)
- 1/2 pound cured ham, diced
- 2 medium white onions, diced
- 4 garlic cloves, minced
- 1 pound dried red beans, picked through and rinsed
- 2 bay leaves
- 2 tablespoons extra-virgin olive oil
- 1 *cubanella* or green bell pepper, chopped (see Note, page 43)
- 1 tablespoon dried Mexican oregano (see Note, page 73)
- 1/2 pound *calabaza*, peeled, cleaned, and cut into 1/2-inch chunks (see Note, page 43)
- 2 medium Idaho potatoes, peeled and cut into 1/2-inch chunks
  Salt and freshly ground black pepper

Melt the lard in a large stockpot over medium heat. Add the ham and cook for 10 minutes to caramelize. Add half of the onions and garlic, and cook, stirring, for 2 minutes to soften. Add the beans, bay leaves, and 2 quarts of cold water. Bring to a boil, cover, reduce the heat to medium-low, and simmer for 1 hour.

Meanwhile, make a *sofrito*: Coat a skillet with the oil and place over medium heat. Add the pepper, oregano, and remaining onions and garlic. Cook, stirring, for 10 minutes, until the vegetables have softened; don't let them brown. Transfer the *sofrito* to a blender and purée until smooth (if necessary, add a little water to help get it going). Pour the *sofrito* purée into the beans. Add the *calabaza* and potatoes, and season with salt and pepper to taste. Cook for 30 minutes, until the mixture is thick and the vegetables are tender.

FRÍJOLES **BORRACHOS**

{drunken beans}

Although beans have no border per se, generally pinto beans are preferred in northern Mexico and south Texas, while black beans are favored in the southern regions of Mexico and all over Guatemala. Literally speaking *borracho* means "drunken," but in the culinary sense it refers to a number of traditional Mexican dishes that are cooked with alcohol, beer, or tequila. *¡Que rico!* Mexican cowboys, *vaqueros, or charros,* are renowned for a similar pinto bean dish called ranch beans or cowboy-style beans— *frijoles charros.* Dried pinto beans tend to be quite dirty, so it's important to wash and scrub them really well. Creaming the beans adds body to the broth.

SERVES 6 TO 8

1 pound dried pinto beans, picked through and well washed
2 bay leaves
1 medium white onion, diced
2 garlic cloves, minced
2 ripe tomatoes, coarsely chopped
1 pickled jalapeño, sliced (see Note, page 139)
1 tablespoon dried Mexican oregano (see Note, page 73)
1 12-ounce bottle dark beer, such as Negra Modelo
Salt and freshly ground black pepper

Put the beans and bay leaves in a large pot, cover with 2 quarts of cold water, and place over medium heat. Cover and simmer for 1 hour.

Add the onion, garlic, tomatoes, jalapeño, oregano, and beer. If necessary, add more water to keep the beans covered. Simmer, covered, until the beans are tender, about another 30 minutes. The mixture should be brothy, but not as loose as a soup.

Ladle out 2 cups of the beans and purée in a blender. Return the puréed beans to the pot to thicken the broth. (You can also "cream the beans," as they say, by mashing a few times with a potato masher.) Stir, and season with salt and pepper to taste.

PURÉ DE **BONIATO**

{mashed boniato}

This is the Latino answer to garlic mashed potatoes. I like to serve this with pork because the creaminess and sweetness of the *boniato* cuts the fattiness and saltiness of the meat.

SERVES 4

- 1 pound *boniato* (see Note)
- 1 pint heavy cream
- 5 garlic cloves
- 2 tablespoons (¼ stick) unsalted butter, at room temperature
- Salt and freshly ground black pepper

Fill a large pot with 1 quart of cold water. Peel and cut the *boniato* into even-sized chunks; put the pieces in the water (this keeps them from oxidizing from the air). Add the heavy cream and garlic. Bring to a boil, uncovered. Simmer until there is no resistance when a fork is inserted into the *boniato*, 20 to 25 minutes.

Reserve 1 cup of the creamy cooking water, then drain the *boniato* and garlic in a colander. Place both in a large bowl while still hot, pour in the reserved cream-water, and pulverize with a potato masher. Add the butter and salt and pepper to taste. Mash until the mixture is creamy and lump-free.

BONIATO

Also called *batata*, white yam, and Cuban sweet potato. The *boniato* is a root vegetable grown in the Caribbean, with a flavor similar to that of a sweet potato, yet drier and starchier; the sweet white flesh has the essence of chestnut. It's about the size of a turnip, with an outer thin skin that can be seen in a rainbow of colors, such as pink, purple, and red.

GUINEOS VERDES CON MOJO

{green bananas with citrus-garlic sauce}

This is a real stick-to-your-ribs dish that is a derivative of *mangu*, Dominican-style boiled and mashed green plantains. Mashed bananas are a satisfying morning meal, historically fed to field-workers before they went out to work a long day. It also makes a creamy side dish that pairs nicely with assertive meats like pork and beef. *Fufu* is Cuba's version of mashed sweet plantains, with bits of crispy bacon and onions mixed in. In this Cuban-influenced recipe, hot *mojo* is poured over the steaming *guineos*, so the garlic bits adhere and the heat produces a crisp coating.

SERVES 4

1   tablespoon salt
4   *guineos* or green bananas, peeled and halved (see Note)
1   recipe hot Mojo (page 233)

Bring a pot of water to a boil over high heat and add the salt. Add the prepared *guineos* and boil for 15 minutes, until very soft. Drain and put in a serving bowl. Pour the hot *mojo* over the steaming *guineos* so it sears a garlic crust. Serve immediately.

GUINEOS

Also referred to as "finger bananas" because of their shape and size. They are much smaller and creamier than their big cousin, the green plantain. Because these green bananas are so petite, they tend to be on the sweeter side. But like plantains, they must be cooked before eating.

To peel *guineos*, score the skin lengthwise and submerge them under boiling water for 20 minutes, or until the skin turns black. Drain the *guineos* and allow them to cool slightly. Carefully run your thumb up the slits and the skin should peel away easily. Cut as directed in the recipe.

FRÍJOLES NEGROS **REFRITOS**

{refried black beans}

Beans are an indispensable staple in the Mexican home and served at every meal because they are cheap, filling, and a good source of vegetarian protein. Inevitably, there are always leftover beans hanging around the kitchen, hence the need to find new and different ways of using them up; that's how *refritos* was born. *Refrito* does not translate as "twice fried" but "fried well." A pot of beans takes on a new form when mashed and cooked until the liquid concentrates and the beans thicken up. They're used as a component in many recipes, such as the *Torta de Huevo y Chorizo* (page 87), and as a side sprinkled with cheese and served with rice and fried plantains. The small, distinctively flavored black turtle beans are prized in southern Mexico and Veracruz because of their high quality and tenderness. I always use dried beans, because in my experience canned beans don't suck up the other flavors as well and lose precious nutrients. Many cooks include pieces of bacon or chorizo to flavor the beans; it's a personal choice, but I believe these meats' salty-smoky flavor overwhelms the creamy taste of the beans.

MAKES 1 QUART, SERVES 4

1 pound dried black turtle beans, picked through and rinsed
2 bay leaves
1 tablespoon dried Mexican oregano (see Note, page 73)
¼ cup lard (page 224)
1 medium white onion, chopped
2 garlic cloves, minced
1 jalapeño, minced
1 teaspoon ground coriander
1 teaspoon ground cumin
1 teaspoon sugar
 Salt and freshly ground black pepper to taste

Put the beans, bay leaves, and oregano in a pot, cover with 2 quarts of cold water, and place over medium heat. Cover and simmer for 2 hours, until the beans are very tender; you want to cook them to the point where they start bursting and are almost overcooked. Mash the beans, along with the liquid in the pot, with the back of a wooden spoon or potato masher to a coarse purée.

Melt the lard in a deep skillet over medium-high heat until it's rippling. Add the onion, garlic, jalapeño, coriander, cumin, and sugar; stir for 2 minutes, until fragrant. Add the mashed beans and continue cooking and stirring for 5 minutes to evaporate some but not all of the liquid; they should be moist and creamy, not dry. Watch the heat carefully to prevent the beans from sticking and burning. Season with salt and pepper before serving.

THE MISSION'S SALVADOREAN FOOD

One rainy San Francisco day, my girlfriend, Glenda, and I discovered a little gem on the outskirts of the Mission. In Diamond Heights across from Cesar Chavez is a great *pupusería* with not much in the way of décor, but a welcoming sight nonetheless: As you enter, you immediately notice women preparing *pupusas* to order. You choose from different cheeses and other fillings, which are spread so evenly that the large amount of dough seems in perfect proportion. I was so impressed by their handiwork that I wanted to jump behind the counter and join them, but Glenda secured us a table amid the families and other large groups. We spent the evening eating from large plates of *pupusas* accompanied by small salads and rice and beans, and listening to the jukebox's great selection of Latin classics and new beats; by the time we left, the rain had long ended.

FRITURAS DE **YUCA**

These delicious *cuchifritos*, or "little fried things," are the Cuban equivalent of hush puppies—eaten as a side dish or just as a great nosh.

SERVES 4

1 pound yuca, peeled and cut into large chunks
3 tablespoons extra-virgin olive oil
4 scallions, white and green parts, chopped
2 garlic cloves, minced
2 large eggs
1 tablespoon chopped flat-leaf parsley
¼ teaspoon baking powder
    Salt and freshly ground black pepper
1 medium red onion, thinly sliced
¼ cup red wine vinegar
1 teaspoon dried Mexican oregano (see Note, page 73)
    Canola oil for frying

Boil the yuca in a pot of salted water over medium heat until tender but not soggy, approximately 20 minutes; be sure not to overcook. Drain, remove the stringy center, and set aside to cool to room temperature.

Coat a small skillet with 1 tablespoon of the oil and place over medium heat. Add the scallions and garlic and sauté for 3 minutes to soften, then set aside to cool.

In a food processor, combine the eggs, parsley, baking powder, and the cooled scallion-garlic mixture. Purée until smooth, then season with 1 teaspoon each of salt and pepper. Add the cooled yuca and purée again until thoroughly combined; it should look like cake batter.

To make the pickled red onions, coat the same small skillet with the remaining 2 tablespoons of oil and put back on medium heat. Add the red onion, vinegar, and oregano and cook for 5 minutes, until the onion is soft. Season to taste with additional salt and pepper and set aside to cool.

In a large skillet, heat 2 inches of oil to 375°F. (Check the temperature with an instant-read thermometer or sprinkle some flour in the hot oil; if it sizzles, the oil is ready.) Using an ice cream scooper or two spoons, carefully drop balls of the yuca batter into the hot oil; do not overcrowd the pan. Fry the fritters for 1 minute on each side, until golden, then drain on paper towels. Season with salt and pepper while still hot, and top with a spoonful of pickled onions.

PLÁTANOS RELLENOS

{stuffed plantains}

Plantains and cheese are a frequently seen combination of flavors; the salty cheese and sweet plantains balance each other out. This dish makes an impressive first course or serves as a side to succulent meats; roasting and stuffing the plantains is a nice alternative to the ever-popular fried version. Carving out little canoes to hold the savory stuffing adds to the overall flavor punch, not to mention that the presentation is cool, too. Be imaginative with the stuffing—basically, any filling recipe from this book will work, but especially good are *Picadillo* (page 117), pork filling from *pasteles* (page 82), and *Carne con Chile Colorado* (page 114). At Paladar, roasted plantain-boats packed sky-high with *bacalao* are one of our biggest hits.

SERVES 4

4 ripe black (sweet) plantains (see Note, page 153)
2 cups Refried Black Beans (page 166)
1 cup crumbled *queso fresco* (see Note, page 75)
1/2 cup *crema fresca* or sour cream

Preheat the oven to 400°F.

Trim the ends of the plantains and make a slit down the seam of the skin so steam can escape during cooking. Wrap the plantains in aluminum foil, place directly on the middle rack of the oven, and bake for 20 minutes. The flesh should be soft and creamy and the skin should pull away. You can also roast on an outdoor grill.

Unwrap the plantains and let them cool for a few minutes. Carefully peel off the skin, keeping the soft flesh intact. Run a knife down the length of the plantain to make an incision, but do not cut all the way through. Use your fingers to open up the cavity. Fill each plantain boat with 1/2 cup of hot refried beans, 1/4 cup of crumbled *queso*, and a tablespoon or two of *crema fresca*. Serve immediately, while the cheese and cream are melting.

SOPA SECA DE **FIDEOS**

Though many people don't associate pasta with Mexican cooking, *fideos* are a favorite. I have fond memories of my mother making this for me when I was growing up. The great thing about this dish is the technique of browning the pasta in oil—toasting adds nuttiness. Typically, coiled nests of vermicelli are fried, then broken up in pieces. But I don't like the texture of these thin noodles for this dish; I prefer small shapes such as alphabet pasta, tiny tubes, or melon seeds (orzo). *Sopa seca* is translated as "dry soup," because all the broth absorbs into the pasta; serve it as a side dish in place of rice. For an appetizer, don't cook it down completely, but leave it a little brothy. Add seafood or shredded chicken for a more substantial meal.

SERVES 4

1 medium white onion, peeled and halved
2 garlic cloves, peeled
1 large tomato
1 jalapeño
¼ cup extra-virgin olive oil
1 cup coarsely chopped cilantro
1 teaspoon dried Mexican oregano (see Note, page 73)
¼ cup vegetable oil
1 7-ounce package Mexican *fideos* pasta, such as alphabet or melon seeds
2 cups Chicken Broth (page 227)
  Salt and freshly ground black pepper
1 cup grated *Cotija* or Parmesan cheese

Put a dry skillet over a medium-high flame and let it get nice and hot, a good 2 minutes. Rub the onion, garlic, tomato, and jalapeño with 1 tablespoon of the oil. Lay the vegetables in the hot pan and roast, turning occasionally, until soft and well charred on all sides, about 10 minutes. Allow the vegetables to cool. Peel the skin from the jalapeño and remove the stem. Put the charred vegetables in a blender, along with the cilantro and oregano. Purée until completely smooth.

Place a pot over medium heat and add the remaining oil. When the oil begins to smoke, add the pasta. Stir constantly until the pasta is golden, about 2 minutes. Pour in the vegetable purée and the broth, and season with salt and pepper to taste. Bring to a boil and simmer for 5 minutes, stirring frequently, until the noodles are tender and the liquid is absorbed. Sprinkle with the cheese before serving.

PAPAS CHORREADAS

Peruvians first cultivated potatoes, and they're still widely used in South American cooking. These Colombian-style creamed potatoes are commonly served with grilled butterflied steak (page 122) as part of a mixed grill or with *Sancocho* (page 42). The roasted poblano is my own addition—it reminds me of the peppers in *Tamales de Rajas* (page 84).

SERVES 4

1 pound Red Bliss potatoes, halved

1 tablespoon salt

2 *poblano* peppers (see Note, page 85)

3 tablespoons extra-virgin olive oil

1 medium white onion, thinly sliced

2 garlic cloves, minced

1 ripe tomato, thinly sliced

1 pint heavy cream

1 cup grated *queso blanco* or Jack cheese (see Note, page 75)

Freshly ground black pepper

1/2 cup chopped cilantro

Put the potatoes in a pot of water, add the salt, and bring to a boil. Cook until fork-tender, about 30 minutes. Drain and set aside.

Meanwhile, rub the *poblanos* with 1 tablespoon of oil, and roast the peppers on a very hot grill, over a gas flame, or under a broiler until the skin is blistered and blackened on all sides. Put the peppers in a bowl, cover with plastic wrap, and let sweat for about 10 minutes to loosen the skins. Peel and rub off the charred skin, pull out the cores, and remove the seeds. Cut the peppers into 1/4-inch strips.

In a deep skillet or pot, heat the remaining 2 tablespoons of oil over a medium flame. Add the onion, garlic, and tomato; cook for 5 minutes, until soft. Add the *poblano* strips and sauté for 2 minutes to combine. Add the drained potatoes, tossing to coat them in the pepper mixture. Pour in the cream and cook, stirring, for 2 minutes, until steam rises from the pan. Remove the pan from the heat and fold in the cheese until melted, thick, and creamy; season with additional salt and pepper to taste. Pour the creamy potatoes onto a serving platter and garnish with the cilantro.

CALABACITAS CON PICO DE GALLO

{sautéed zucchini with fresh salsa}

Calabacitas are Mexican zucchini that are light in color and egg shaped; if you can get your hands on them, use them. If not, Italian zucchini or yellow squash works also. This recipe stems from a traditional Mexican dish called *calabacitas*, which is a combination of zucchini, onion, tomato, and cheese. I simplify it here by cooking the zucchini with the vegetable salsa *pico de gallo*, which is normally served raw.

SERVES 4

2 tablespoons extra-virgin olive oil
1 *chile de árbol,* minced (see Note, page 231)
1 garlic clove, minced
1 pound zucchini, cut into ¼-inch circles
1 recipe *Pico de Gallo* (page 234)
½ cup *queso blanco* (see Note, page 75)

Place a deep skillet over medium heat and coat with the oil. Add the chile and garlic and stir for 1 minute to flavor the oil. Add the zucchini and sauté for 3 minutes to soften. Add the *Pico de Gallo,* and continue to cook until the tomatoes begin to break down and the mixture is heated through, about 5 minutes. Remove from the heat, fold in the cheese, and serve.

ELOTES ASADOS

{roasted corn with chile-lime butter}

This is my version of the popular street food *esquites*, roasted corn that's sold from bicycle carts and eaten as a snack during an evening stroll through town. It's also a welcome addition to any barbecue.

SERVES 4

4 ears fresh corn, unhusked

½ cup (1 stick) unsalted butter, at room temperature

Juice of 2 limes

1 canned *chipotle* in adobo, finely chopped

1 teaspoon ground cumin

2 garlic cloves, minced

2 tablespoons finely chopped cilantro

1 teaspoon salt

½ teaspoon freshly ground black pepper

Preheat the oven to 350°F.

Place the corn, in its husks, directly on the center rack of the oven (you can also roast the corn on an outdoor grill). Roast for 20 minutes, until the corn is soft when you press on it.

In the meantime, prepare the chile-lime butter: In a medium bowl, combine the butter with the lime juice, *chipotle*, cumin, garlic, cilantro, salt, and pepper. Mix well to combine thoroughly.

To finish off the corn, peel down the husks, remove the corn silk, and tie the husks in a knot so you can hold onto it like a handle. Char the corn on a hot grill, over a gas flame, or under a broiler, until the kernels are slightly blackened all around and start popping, about 6 minutes. Serve with a spoonful of the chile-lime butter melting over the kernels.

QUELITES

{sautéed greens}

Specifically, *quelites* is the Mexican green lamb's quarters, a dark jagged-leafed green that's the cousin of the herb epazote. In the common vernacular, though, *quelites* can mean a variety of greens, including spinach; I favor the pungent peppery bite of mustard greens, but any dark leafy green will work. The nutritious grassy broth is almost medicinal. Serve with *Pollo Borracho* (page 145).

SERVES 4

¼ cup extra-virgin olive oil
2 garlic cloves, slivered
1 medium white onion, diced
1 ripe tomato, chopped
2 pounds mustard greens, kale, or Swiss chard, washed and stemmed
1 cup Chicken Broth (page 227)
Juice of 1 lemon
Salt and freshly ground black pepper

Place a large pot or deep skillet over medium heat and coat with the oil. Add the garlic and cook slowly for 2 minutes, or until golden but not brown. Add the onion and cook for 2 minutes to sweat. Add the tomato and cook for a minute to break it down. Add the greens in batches, turning them over so they wilt; keep adding more handfuls as there's room in the pot. Pour in the broth and cook the liquid down by half, about 5 minutes. Squeeze in the lemon to brighten the flavor, and season with salt and pepper to taste.

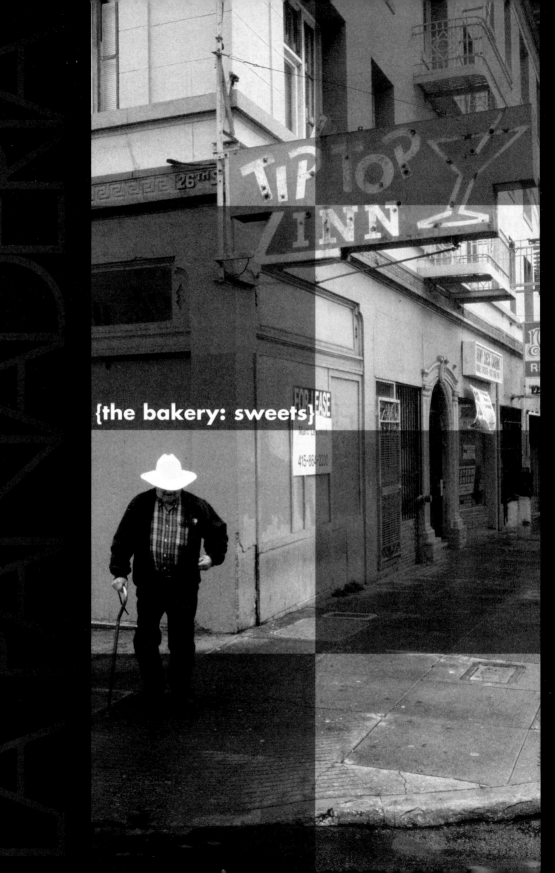

{the bakery: sweets}

DULCE DE LECHE
{milk caramel}

SIROPE DE PILONCILLO
{piloncillo syrup}

FLAN DE COCO
{coconut caramel custard}

CAMOTES Y PLÁTANOS ASADOS
{roasted sweet plantains
and sweet potatoes}

NATILLA DE PIÑA
{pineapple pudding}

PIÑA ASADA
{broiled pineapple}

ARROZ DULCE
{rice pudding}

CAPIROTADA
{bread pudding}

TRES LECHES
{three-milks cake}

EMPANADAS DE GUAYABA Y QUESO
{guava and cheese turnovers}

BUÑUELOS
{crisps}

CHURROS CON SALSA DE CHOCOLATE
{cinnamon doughnuts with
chocolate dunking sauce}

MERENGUES
{meringues}

POLVORONES
{crumb cookies}

BIZCOCHO DE CALABAZA
{pumpkin cake}

BIZCOCHO DE CHOCOLATE
{chocolate cake}

I SUPPOSE THAT BAKERIES ARE beloved every-

where in the world, but I think that Latins hold a special place in their hearts for the *panadería,* a place where you get sweet breads for breakfast, tremendous multitiered cakes for weddings, rolls for sandwiches, cookies for snacks. Everything is baked on the premises—Latins aren't big on centralized commissary-type operations. The bins of baked goods are arranged around the floor of the shop, not hidden behind the counter. When you enter the *panadería,* you grab a plastic tray (think high-school cafeteria) and a pair of long-handled tongs, and you wander around, poking each bin with your tongs, catching a whiff of each treat, picking what you want, and placing it on your tray. Self-restraint is crucial, or you end up with a banquet for twenty instead of breakfast for four; you don't want to bring undisciplined children.

The big cakes—for weddings, birthdays, and other celebrations—are in a different part of the shop, sometimes on a different level—upstairs, where things are more serious. You leave behind the chaotic meandering of the bin-picking, and enter a serene, quiet area with ample space for each spectacular cake to be showcased. It's like leaving the floor of a department store on sale day and entering the bridal boutique.

Many restaurants, especially those on the lower end of things like the *paladars* and *fondas,* don't serve dessert, except maybe a vat of flan that looks prehistoric, or a rice pudding that looks, well, like rice pudding—never beautiful. When you've finished your entrée you may get a coffee, but just as likely you'll simply pay the bill and walk out. If you want dessert, you get it from a bakery—they're open late for this purpose—and you bring it home. Again, this is the Latin sense of doing most of your eating at home: You may go to a *taquería* for quick sustenance, but for lounging over a pastry, you should be at home.

Or you should be really *out,* in a proper restaurant (a *comedor* or *restaurante*) or a café, where the specialties are baked goods and hot drinks—*chocolate caliente* and various types of coffee. These cafés are similar to European ones, with little tables that don't have room for full dinner plates, no tableclothes, quick service, and an unhurried atmosphere. The café culture is particularly strong in Cuba and other European-influenced Caribbean countries, in the more colonial-oriented cities of Mexico, and especially in Argentina. Wherever you find these immigrants in the United States, you'll find cafés.

But what you won't get at a café, a bakery, or a restaurant of nearly any type is ice cream: For this, you need to go to an ice-cream shop for such remarkable flavors as avocado and cactus-fruit. Here you can also get *helados,* ices that are very similar to sorbet—ice is ready-mixed with flavoring. On the more casual end, you can get *raspadas* on the street—shaved ices, made with a special tool that removes crunchy splinters from a huge block of ice and flavored with syrups like mango, guava, and tamarind. On hot days in barrios all across the United States, you'll find *raspadas* carts wherever you find a lot of people—the ice will probably be hidden beneath a dishtowel of dubious cleanliness, but you'll identify the cart by the dozen or so bottles of vividly colored syrups. (You'll also notice a throng of kids with green and orange tongues standing around, smiling.) Yet another option, also from carts but also sometimes in convenience stores, are the frozen popsicles called *paletas*—again, of the green tongue–producing variety.

The Latin sweet tooth is a very sweet one, and an abundance of sugar is often balanced by extremely tart flavors—a flavor high-wire act, like much of the Latin kitchen: bold, but in balance.

DULCE DE LECHE

Dulce de leche is a Hispanic term for a type of caramel sauce. The silky smooth caramel is made by slowly simmering sweetened milk until it is very thick and amber colored. (*Cajeta* is the Mexican version, made with goat's milk.) The intensely flavored concoction is widely used in Latin America and is the main ingredient in filling most Argentinean pastries and cakes. In the Hispanic home, it is commonly spread on toast and waffles in the morning, stirred into black coffee, and drizzled on fresh fruit for dessert. It's fantastic mixed into some vanilla ice cream (even Häagen-Dazs has caught on to this flavor) or heated slightly and poured on top of a sundae. *Dulce de leche* can be found commercially in Latin markets, but the products usually contain corn syrup and a bunch of other unnecessary additives. This recipe is easy: You just have to keep an eye on maintaining the water level in the double boiler (gently heating in a double boiler prevents scorching). A common practice among Latin chefs (myself included) is to place the *unopened* cans of milk directly in a pot of water to cover. But simmering the condensed milk inside its container for hours presents a potentially dangerous situation due to expansion and pressure, so I do not recommend this procedure. Stored in a covered container in the refrigerator, the sauce keeps for one month.

MAKES ABOUT 3 CUPS

2 14-ounce cans sweetened condensed milk

Pour the milk into the top of a double boiler and place over a pot of barely simmering water. Gently simmer for 2 hours over low heat, occasionally stirring with a wooden spoon as the milk thickens. Add more water to the double boiler as it evaporates. The sweetened milk will caramelize to a lovely tannish-brown. Cool to room temperature and then refrigerate until ready to use.

SIROPE DE **PILONCILLO**

{piloncillo syrup}

Piloncillo syrup is a must for the Latin sweet tooth. The sugar is melted down and spiced up, resulting in a delicious mahogany glaze. It is used in *Capirotada* (page 190) and often poured over Rice Pudding (page 189) and *Buñuelos* (page 199), and even on French toast and pancakes. The spicy sugar syrup is also used in many drinks: stirred into iced tea; shaken with rum, lime, and plenty of ice; and mixed into coffee drinks such as *café de olla* and Cuban latte.

MAKES 1 CUP

- 1 8-ounce cone *piloncillo* or 1 cup packed dark brown sugar and 2 tablespoons molasses (see Note, page 33)
- 2 cinnamon sticks, preferably Mexican *canela* (see Note, page 21)
- ¼ teaspoon whole cloves

Grate the cone, starting at the narrow end, with a box grater into a heavy-bottomed pot. Add 2 cups of water, the cinnamon, and cloves; give it a stir and place over medium-high heat. Swirl the pan over the heat until the sugar dissolves to a dark syrup, about 20 minutes.

FLAN DE **COCO**

{coconut caramel custard}

Flan is the silky Spanish custard that gets its richness and yellow color from lots of eggs; the creamy yet gelatinous custard is flavored with caramel. The dish is inverted and the liquefied caramel drips over the flan to create a thin, delicious syrup. Velvety flan is a perfect canvas for a dessert lover who enjoys experimenting with an endless bank of accent flavors. I use coconut here, but I also like chocolate, orange, coffee, and cinnamon—just to name a few. Historically, flan was cooked on top of a stove in a water bath. But using a bain-marie and baking in the oven is a standard modern approach. Poaching the custard in the gentle heat of a bath remains the preferred method because of custard's delicate nature (crème brûlée and crème caramel are cooked the same way). The heat can be regulated to keep the water at an even, constant temperature.

SERVES 10

1 3/4 cups sugar
1 tablespoon lemon juice
6 large eggs
3 large egg yolks
1 pint whole milk
1 13 1/2-ounce can unsweetened coconut milk
3 tablespoons light rum (optional)
1/2 cup toasted shredded unsweetened coconut (see Note)

To make the caramel, have ready ten 6-ounce custard cups and a large roasting pan. Combine 1 1/4 cups of the sugar and 1/2 cup of water in a heavy-bottomed pot. Place over medium-high heat and cook until the sugar begins to melt, about 5 minutes; don't stir with a spoon. Add the lemon juice while it is heating; the acid prevents the sugar from crystallizing, keeping the caramel smooth and clear. Swirl the pan over the heat until the syrup darkens to a medium amber color, about 5 minutes. Remove from the heat and immediately divide among the custard cups. Tilt the dishes so that the caramel evenly coats the bottom and a bit of the sides. Place the cups in the roasting pan and set aside.

Preheat the oven to 325°F, and bring a kettle of water to a boil for the water bath and keep it hot.

In a large bowl, cream together the whole eggs and yolks with the remaining ½ cup of sugar. Whisk until the mixture is pale yellow and thick.

Pour the milk and coconut milk (and rum if you are using it) into a saucepan over a medium-low flame. Bring the milk to a brief simmer, stirring occasionally. Take care not to let the milk come to a full boil to prevent overflow. Temper the egg mixture by gradually whisking in the hot milk mixture; don't add it too quickly or the eggs will cook. Pass the mixture through a strainer into a large measuring cup to ensure that the flan will be perfectly smooth. Divide the mixture among the caramel-coated molds.

To create the water bath, pour the hot (not boiling) water into the roasting pan to come halfway up the sides of the ramekins; be careful not to get water into the custard. Carefully transfer to the middle oven rack and bake for 45 minutes, until the custard is barely set and just jiggles slightly. Let the flan cool in the water bath, then refrigerate for at least 4 hours or overnight.

When you are ready to serve, run a knife around the inside of the molds to loosen the flan. Place a dessert plate on top of the flan and invert to pop it out. Garnish with any remaining caramel and the toasted coconut.

TOASTING COCONUT

Preheat the oven to 350°F. Spread the coconut on a cookie sheet and bake for 10 minutes, tossing it halfway through cooking.

CAMOTES Y PLÁTANOS ASADOS

{roasted sweet plantains and sweet potatoes}

On the streets of Mexico City, you'll see big fifty-gallon drums of roasting sweet plantains and potatoes being stoked with wood. Spicy *piloncillo* syrup is poured over the hot starchy vegetables to coat like a glossy lacquer and then eaten on a stick. Variations of this abound in Caribbean and Mexican neighborhoods in the United States, where plantains are readily available.

SERVES 4 TO 8

4 sweet potatoes
4 ripe black (sweet) plantains (see Note, page 153)
1 cup *piloncillo* syrup (page 183)

Preheat the oven to 400°F.

Pierce the sweet potatoes with a fork and place directly on the middle oven rack. Bake until tender, about 1 hour.

To prepare the plantains, trim the ends and make a slit down the seam of the skin so steam can escape during cooking. Wrap the plantains in aluminum foil. Put them in the oven with the potatoes for the last 20 minutes of cooking. Remove the sweet potatoes and plantains from the oven, and unwrap the plantains. Let the potatoes and plantains cool for a few minutes, then carefully peel off the skins. Halve the plantains and sweet potatoes crosswise and put them on a serving platter. Pour the *piloncillo* syrup over the vegetables and discard the cinnamon sticks and cloves.

NATILLA DE PIÑA

Natilla is an egg custard that's eaten all over Latin America, particularly in Cuba and Colombia, and has roots in the Basque dessert sauce that is like the Spanish crème anglaise. This pudding is great by itself or with fruit, such as the Broiled Pineapple (page 188). It takes on flavors very well—substitute orange juice concentrate or banana nectar for the pineapple juice, if desired. Cornstarch is crucial to thickening the pudding; *maizena* is Spanish cornstarch, which comes in different flavors for the purpose of making *natillas*.

SERVES 4 TO 6

2 cups whole milk

½ cup sugar

   Pinch of salt

1 tablespoon cornstarch

¼ cup thawed pineapple juice concentrate

2 large egg yolks, lightly beaten

1 teaspoon freshly grated nutmeg

Combine the milk, sugar, and salt in a pot over medium heat. Bring up to a simmer, stirring occasionally. In a small bowl, dissolve the cornstarch in the pineapple juice, whisk to smooth out the lumps, and then add it to the pot. Continue to simmer and stir until the mixture begins to thicken, about 10 minutes. Add the yolks and bring to a boil, stirring constantly, until the mixture is very thick and puddinglike. Remove immediately and pour into a dessert bowl. Refrigerate for at least 4 hours or overnight. Dust with the nutmeg before serving.

PIÑA ASADA

{broiled pineapple}

This simple preparation is wonderful served hot with *Natilla de Piña* (page 187) spooned in the center of each pineapple ring.

SERVES 4 TO 6 (2 TO 4 RINGS PER SERVING)

1	large ripe pineapple
½	cup sugar
	Finely grated zest of 1 lime
1	teaspoon ground cinnamon, preferably Mexican *canela* (see Note, page 21)
½	cup (1 stick), unsalted butter, melted

Preheat the broiler. Using a large sharp knife, cut off the leaves of the pineapple. Slice off the bottom to stabilize the base and stand the pineapple up. Cut off the rind from top to bottom, removing as much of the eyes as possible. Turn the pineapple on its side and slice crosswise into ½-inch-thick rounds. Cut the core out of each slice with a paring knife. Arrange the pineapple rings on a sheet pan lined with aluminum foil.

In a small bowl, toss together the sugar, lime zest, and cinnamon. Brush the pineapple with the melted butter and sprinkle with the sugar mixture. Broil until caramelized and bubbly, about 2 to 4 minutes.

ARROZ DULCE

{rice pudding}

Rice pudding is the ultimate comfort food; this version has a bit of alcohol for an adult twist (if kids are eating, simply omit soaking the dried fruit in mescal). Also known as *Arroz con Leche,* rice pudding is often eaten at breakfast in the Latin home. Before serving, top with whipped cream or *Dulce de Leche* (page 182) for total indulgence.

SERVES 8

½ cup coarsely chopped dried apricots

½ cup raisins

1 cup mescal or tequila

6 cups whole milk, plus more to taste, chilled

¼ teaspoon salt

1 cinnamon stick, preferably Mexican *canela* (see Note, page 21)

Zest of 1 lime, cut in large strips

1 vanilla bean

1 cup long-grain rice

¾ cup sugar

1 teaspoon ground cinnamon, preferably Mexican *canela*

Combine the apricots and raisins in a large bowl. Add the mescal, turning to coat. Soak the dried fruit for 1 hour to reconstitute. Drain and discard the mescal.

Pour the milk into a large saucepan and place over medium heat. Add the salt, cinnamon stick, and lime zest. Using a paring knife, split the vanilla bean down the middle lengthwise, scrape out the seeds, and add them to the saucepan; toss the pod in there too for good measure. Cover and simmer for 5 minutes to flavor the milk.

Pour in the rice and let the milk return to a boil. When it boils, give it a stir, then cover and cook over medium-low heat for 20 minutes. The rice should be tender but firm, with a fair amount of milk still remaining in the pot.

Uncover and add the sugar. Cook and stir for 20 minutes over a medium-low flame, until the mixture is creamy and starts to thicken; the pudding will continue to firm up as it cools. Remove from the heat. Fish out the cinnamon stick, lime zest, and vanilla bean. Fold in the plumped apricots and raisins. Spoon the pudding into a serving dish and dust with the ground cinnamon. Serve chilled or at room temperature. If chilled, check the consistency before serving and add chilled milk as needed to loosen up the pudding.

CAPIROTADA

This Mexican bread pudding is a traditional dish during Lent, and a favorite of Latin eateries that serve Cuban sandwiches and Mexican tortas. Three-day-old bread can be transformed into a sweet treat—nothing ever goes to waste.

Bolillos are the traditional choice but French bread, brioche, or challah may be substituted. The toasted bread is layered with cheese, nuts, and fruit, with brown sugar syrup poured over it to moisten. This may sound like an odd mingling, but trust me, the mild cheese is not pronounced—it holds the pudding together more than anything. The type of cheese, nuts, and fruits used are subject to the cook's interpretation: Cheddar, peanuts, raisins, and sliced apples are standard choices. To change it up, this recipe uses *queso blanco*, almonds, and a tequila-soaked tropical fruit salsa—very sexy! The salsa is a delicious mixture of tropical fruit and is fabulous on a piece of pound cake or *Buñuelos* (page 199). (If serving children, just omit the tequila and double the orange juice to total 1 cup.) Don't confuse *capirotada* with *budín de pan*, which is a bread pudding much like the American version, made with milk and eggs.

SERVES 8 TO 10

1 large mango, peeled, seeded, and cut into 1-inch cubes

1 medium papaya, peeled, seeded, and cut into 1-inch cubes

½ medium pineapple, peeled, cored, and cut into 1-inch cubes

2 tablespoons sugar

2 tablespoons chopped mint

½ cup tequila

½ cup orange juice

1 1-pound loaf day-old bread, such as *bolillos*, French bread, or brioche, cut into 2-inch cubes

½ cup (1 stick) unsalted butter, melted, plus more for greasing the dish

¾ cup toasted slivered almonds

½ pound grated *queso blanco* (see Note, page 75)

1 recipe *piloncillo* syrup (page 183)

Vanilla ice cream, for serving (optional)

To prepare the fruit salsa, combine the mango, papaya, and pineapple in a large bowl. Sprinkle the fruit with the sugar and mint. Add the tequila and orange juice, toss to coat, and let it macerate for 1 hour.

Meanwhile, preheat the oven to 350°F.

Place the bread cubes in a large mixing bowl. Drizzle ½ cup of melted butter over the cubes, tossing to coat thoroughly. Spread the bread cubes out on a sheet pan and bake for 15 minutes, until dry and lightly golden.

Generously butter the bottom and sides of a 13 × 9-inch baking dish. Layer half of the ingredients in the following order: toasted bread cubes, almonds, fruit salsa, and cheese. Pour 1 cup of the syrup evenly over the cheese. Repeat the layers, finishing with a layer of cheese. Cover the pan with aluminum foil and bake for 30 minutes. Remove the foil and continue to bake for another 10 minutes to brown the top. Serve with vanilla ice cream if desired.

TRES LECHES

{three-milks cake}

Tres Leches is one of the most luscious desserts ever invented. The sponge cake is soaked with three different kinds of milk (whole, evaporated, and condensed), making it incredibly moist and rich. As if *that* wasn't enough, the cake is then frosted with meringue or whipped cream to top it off. I infuse coffee into the milk trio to take it to another level; it's like sopping up melted coffee ice cream with soft vanilla cake! Orange or banana liqueur are other options in place of the coffee. But I must warn you: This is not for the calorie-conscious or lactose-intolerant. On the other hand, at least the cake doesn't have any butter (except to grease the pan). *Tres Leches* is actually Nicaraguan in origin, but has been adopted by many Cuban and Mexican restaurants. In fact, it appears on just about every Cuban menu in Miami, and in the past few years has risen to stardom as the special-occasion cake in Mexico. It's seen in bakeries as a sheet cake or layered with whipped cream. This recipe may seem long and complicated, but it really is a snap to make.

SERVES 8 TO 10

CAKE

- 1 tablespoon unsalted butter, for greasing the baking dish
- 1 cup all-purpose flour, plus more for dusting the baking dish
- 1 1/2 teaspoons baking powder
- 5 large eggs, separated, at room temperature
  Pinch of salt
- 1 cup sugar
- 1 teaspoon vanilla extract

MILK MIXTURE

- 1 14-ounce can sweetened condensed milk
- 1 12-ounce can evaporated milk
- 1 cup whole milk or heavy cream
- 1/2 cup cold brewed espresso or strong coffee

MERINGUE TOPPING

- 1 cup sugar
- 1/2 teaspoon cream of tartar
- 4 large egg whites, at room temperature
- 1 teaspoon vanilla extract

To prepare the cake, butter the bottom of a 13 × 9-inch baking dish. Cut a piece of parchment paper to fit the dish and press it in place. Butter and flour the parchment paper and set aside.

Preheat the oven to 350°F.

In a medium bowl, sift together the remaining 1 cup of flour and the baking powder. In another large bowl, combine the egg whites and salt. Using an electric mixer, beat the egg whites until frothy. Gradually add the sugar, continuing to beat until stiff peaks form. Add the yolks, one at a time, beating well after each addition. Stir in the vanilla. Sift in one-third of the flour mixture, stir, and fold in the remaining flour mixture with a rubber spatula just until incorporated. Be delicate—you don't want to lose the volume of the beaten eggs. Pour the batter into the prepared dish. Bake for 20 to 25 minutes, until the cake springs back when lightly pressed and a toothpick inserted in the center comes out clean.

Cool the cake for 20 minutes. Carefully turn out onto a wire rack and peel off the parchment paper. Return the cake to the pan and pierce the top all over with a fork, so the milk mixture can really penetrate. Allow the cake to cool completely.

To prepare the milk mixture, in a mixing bowl, whisk together the condensed milk, evaporated milk, whole milk, and coffee until well blended. Very slowly, pour the milk mixture evenly over the cooled cake, being sure to get in the corners. Let the cake drink in the liquid before adding more; you may not need all of it. Cover loosely with plastic wrap and refrigerate at least 2 hours or overnight (preferred) to absorb.

To make the meringue, place all but 2 tablespoons of the sugar in a small saucepan with ¼ teaspoon of the cream of tartar and ½ cup water. Bring to a boil, and cook until it becomes a soft ball. In an electric mixer, beat the egg whites with the remaining ¼ teaspoon cream of tartar and remaining 2 tablespoons of sugar. Pour in the reserved sugar mixture in a steady stream while whipping on medium speed; increase the speed to high and whip until the mixture is cooled. Using a wet spatula, spread the top of the cake with a thick layer of the meringue. Refrigerate the cake for at least 1 hour. When ready to serve, cut the cake into squares and serve on small plates so the milk can pool on the bottom.

VARIATION

For *Cuatro Leches*, top the cake with *Dulce de Leche* (page 182) instead of meringue.

EMPANADAS DE **GUAYABA** Y **QUESO**

{guava and cheese turnovers}

Empanadas are most often thought of as little meat pies in traditional Argentinean cuisine. But guava and cheese empanadas are the snack of choice enjoyed alongside Cuban coffee in the Calle Ocho district. These turnovers can be baked (*al horno*) or fried (*fritas*) and stuffed with most any sweet or savory filling—making them perfect for leftovers. The only caveat is that the filling should be moist, but not too wet, to prevent the pastry from becoming soggy and tearing open. Stuff with the chorizo and potato filling (page 91; great for brunch) or the *Picadillo* (page 117); try mashed sweet potatoes or pumpkin with cinnamon. I like to use a fork to crimp the dough because it gives a better seal than pressing by hand. These flaky half-moons of puffed pastry are convenient for quick lunches because they can be eaten with one hand. I easily can knock off six of these little gems as a light meal, or three or four as a snack! Empanadas are also perfect hors d'oeuvres because they can be made in advance and frozen. After cooking, dust sweet empanadas with confectioners' sugar or season savory ones with salt and pepper.

MAKES 12

- 2 cups all-purpose flour, plus more for the counter
- 1 teaspoon salt
- 1/2 cup vegetable shortening
- 1 recipe Guava and Cheese Filling (page 196)
- 1 large egg beaten with 1 tablespoon water, for the egg wash

In a large bowl, combine the flour and salt and sift thoroughly. Cut in the shortening with a pastry blender or rub with your fingers until it looks like fine crumbs. Gradually add 1/2 cup of water to form the dough into a ball; it should be easy to handle and not sticky. Wrap the dough in plastic and chill for 30 minutes.

Lightly flour your rolling pin and counter. Roll the dough to 1/8-inch thickness. Using a 3-inch cookie or biscuit cutter, cut out 12 circles.

Spoon 1 generous tablespoon of the filling into the center of each pastry circle, leaving a 1/2-inch border. Brush the edges with the egg wash and then fold the dough over in half to enclose the filling and form a semicircle. Seal the edges by crimping with the tines of a fork. Chill at least 30 minutes before frying or baking; the turnovers may be stored in a plastic container and frozen at this point.

TO FRY: Heat 2 inches of canola oil in a wide pot or deep skillet to 375°F. (Check the temperature with an instant-read thermometer or sprinkle some flour in the hot oil; if it sizzles, the oil is ready.) Carefully slide the turnovers into the hot oil and fry until they are puffed and crisp, turning to brown evenly, about 5 to 7 minutes. Remove them to a platter lined with paper towels to drain.

TO FRY FROZEN EMPANADAS: Thaw for 30 minutes before frying as above.

TO BAKE: Preheat the oven to 350°F. Place the empanadas on a baking sheet and brush with additional egg wash. Using a fork, prick a few holes in the top of the empanadas for steam to escape. Bake for 30 minutes, until the pastry is golden. Cool slightly and serve warm.

TO BAKE FROZEN EMPANADAS: Preheat the oven to 400°F. Place the frozen turnovers (no need to thaw) on a cooking sheet and brush with the egg wash. Using a paring knife, make 3 small slits in the top of the empanadas for steam to escape. Bake for 30 to 35 minutes, until the pastry is golden and the filling is hot. Cool slightly and serve warm.

dulce de guayaba y queso

{guava and cheese filling}

Guavas are indigenous to the Caribbean, and preferred by Puerto Ricans in many of their traditional dishes. Often guava paste is sliced and served with cream cheese and crackers as a snack in Cuba. It is also a favorite empanada filling, as here. Using guavas in various stages of ripeness gives a complex sweet-tartness to the filling. The natural pectin from the seeds and skin of the guava act as a gel, making it a favorite fruit for marmalades, jams, and jellies. Guava jelly is also a favorite in Jamaica and the title of a famous Bob Marley song.

MAKES 1 QUART

2 pounds guavas, in various stages of ripeness (see Note)
2 cups sugar (approximately)
   Juice of 1 lime
   Finely grated zest of 1 orange
1 4-ounce package cream cheese, at room temperature
1 cup grated *queso blanco* (see Note, page 75)

To make the guava marmalade, wash the guavas well and remove the stems. Chop up the guavas and place in a large pot. Cover with ½ cup of water and boil until they are mushy, about 10 minutes.

Mash the boiled fruit with a potato masher and press the pulp through a strainer to remove the seeds. Measure the guava purée; for each cup of purée, add an equal amount of sugar (you should have about 2 cups). Put the guava purée, sugar, lime juice, and orange zest in the pot and place over medium-low heat. Simmer to dissolve the sugar, stirring constantly. The marmalade should be thick enough to coat the back of a spoon. Allow to cool to room temperature.

To prepare the rest of the filling, mix together the softened cream cheese and grated cheese until semismooth. Fold in the guava marmalade to combine.

GUAVAS

A sweet, tropical fruit that is native to the Caribbean and grows domestically in the warm climates of California, Florida, and Hawaii; the major worldwide producers are India, Brazil, and Mexico. Guavas range in size from a lime to an orange and have a thin, edible skin that varies in color as they ripen from yellow to red and eventually to purple-black. Inside, the flesh is pale yellow to salmon-colored and contains tiny, edible seeds. Guavas taste like a cross between a strawberry, with a hint of lemon; their flavor goes from sour to sweet as they ripen. Guavas emit a sweet, pungent fragrance and should be semifirm and free of bruises. As with all tropical fruit, do not store them in the refrigerator. Guavas are considered one of the most nutritious fruits because of their high levels of vitamin C and iron.

Feijoa, guava's green brother, tastes like pineapple and is therefore called pineapple guava.

THE MÉXICO LINDO BAKERY

On 116th Street and Second Avenues, in the heart of New York City's Spanish Harlem, is my favorite bakery in the city's barrio: México Lindo. When I first walked into the place a decade ago, I thought I'd been transported back in time and place to my childhood in El Paso—or, more exactly, to a bakery across the border in Juarez: Before my eyes were the same breads and cookies I'd salivated over as a kid. México Lindo bakes everything on the premises, and there are often long lines for birthday and wedding cakes, as well as for savory treats—they have a small selection of tamales, stuffed with either poblano strips, chicken, or beef, as well as *tortas* and tacos.

But it's not just the food itself that's so evocative of Mexico: It's the setting. México Lindo provides you with tongs and bright-orange plastic trays so you can walk around the shop picking up whatever you choose, cafeteria-style— the same scene you'll see throughout Latin America. In traditional American bakeries, the customers point to what they want, and the person behind the counter snaps it up. This setup is undoubtedly more sanitary than having the customers rummaging around in bins of rolls, but it's a hell of a lot less fun.

BUÑUELOS

{crisps}

These sugar-sprinkled fried cookies are traditionally made for Christmas and New Year's in Latin America. At fiestas, you also see *buñuelos* dusted with confectioners' or cinnamon-sugar and sold in bags of a dozen. Another favorite way to serve these crunchy treats is to break up the cookies into a large soup bowl and top with warm *Dulce de Leche* (page 182), *Piloncillo* Syrup (page 183), or Chocolate Dunking Sauce (page 201). The Cuban version is called *Buñuelos Criollos;* instead of using flour, the dough is made from boiled and mashed starchy vegetables, such as yuca and malanga.

MAKES 24

2 cups all-purpose flour
1 tablespoon sugar
¼ teaspoon baking powder
½ teaspoon salt
1 large egg
¼ cup whole milk
2 tablespoons (¼ stick) unsalted butter, melted
Vegetable oil for frying

Sift the flour, sugar, baking powder, and salt in a large bowl. In a small bowl, whisk the egg and milk together; add it to the dry ingredients. Pour in the melted butter and mix until the dough can be easily handled without being sticky; add 1 or 2 more tablespoons of flour if necessary.

Turn the dough out on a lightly floured surface and knead until very smooth. Divide the dough into about 24 pieces and shape into walnut-size balls. Cover them with a cloth and let rest for about 20 minutes. On a lightly floured surface, roll each ball into a thin, 4-inch circle (about the size of a tortilla). Let the dough rest for 5 minutes.

Pour 1 inch of oil into a large deep skillet and heat to 375°F. (Check the temperature with an instant-read thermometer or sprinkle some flour in the hot oil, if it sizzles, the oil is ready.) Carefully place 2 *buñuelos* at a time in the oil. Fry until the underside is lightly browned, 30 seconds to 1 minute, then turn with tongs and fry the other side for another 30 seconds to 1 minute, until puffed. Drain the *buñuelos* on paper towels, and top with cinnamon-sugar, *piloncillo* syrup, or chocolate sauce.

CHURROS CON SALSA DE CHOCOLATE

{cinnamon doughnuts with chocolate dunking sauce}

Churros are made with a piece of equipment called a *churrera*, a type of pastry tube with a wooden plunger that extrudes the dough into sticks. If you don't have one, use a heavy-duty cloth pastry bag or cookie gun with a large (⅜-inch) star tip. The trick to good *churros* is in the oil temperature: I've found the most success frying at a relatively low temperature of 325°F., so the outside of the *churro* doesn't burn before the inside is cooked.

MAKES 24 CHURROS

- 4 tablespoons (½ stick) unsalted butter
- 2 tablespoons vegetable oil, plus more for deep-frying
- ¼ teaspoon salt
- 2 cups all-purpose flour
- 2 large eggs
- ¼ cup sugar
- 1 teaspoon ground cinnamon, preferably Mexican *canela*
  Salsa de Chocolate (recipe follows)

To make the dough, combine 2 cups of water with the butter, 2 tablespoons oil, and the salt in a saucepan. Bring to a boil over medium-high heat. Add the flour all at once and stir vigorously with a wooden spoon until a ball forms, about 1 minute; remove from heat and let cool slightly in the pot.

Place the dough in a mixer bowl and beat on medium speed with the paddle attachment until no longer hot to the touch. Beat in the eggs, one at a time, until the dough is very smooth and shiny.

Heat 2 inches of oil in a wide pot or deep skillet to 350°F. Spoon the batter into a pastry bag fitted with a star tip. Carefully squeeze 5-inch logs of dough into the hot oil, pinching the dough off the bottom of the bag with your fingers or snipping with scissors. (To get fancy you can also pipe out spiral coils.) Fry only 3 or 4 pieces at a time so the oil temperature stays constant, keeping them away from the sides of the pot so they don't stick. Fry until the *churros* puff up, about 2 minutes on each side, turning once. The inside should be soft but not doughy and the outside crispy-golden. Transfer the *churros* to a platter lined with paper towels to drain. Mix the sugar and cinnamon and spread it out on a plate. Roll the warm *churros* in the cinnamon-sugar, and serve with the *Salsa de Chocolate*.

salsa de chocolate

dunking sauce} {chocolate

MAKES 2 CUPS

2 cups whole milk

¼ cup sugar

3 ounces Mexican or bittersweet chocolate, grated (see Note)

Place the milk and sugar in a saucepan over medium-low heat. Add the chocolate, stirring constantly, until the chocolate has melted, about 10 minutes. Remove from the heat and whisk to smooth it out. Serve in cups for dunking the *churros*.

MEXICAN CHOCOLATE

As far back as anthropologists can determine, the pre-Hispanic civilizations established in Mexico were the first to use the divine cacao tree as an integral part of their culture. The Aztec settlers were followers of the practice inherited by the Mayas, who a long time before used cacao beans as currency and food. Though the methods and ingredients have changed over time, today chocolate has become one of the favorite pleasures around the planet.

Mexican chocolate is an integral part of the Latin kitchen. Every town has a *molino*, a place where locals grind cacao beans with sugar and cinnamon. The chocolate is then formed into containers or into molds and sold in scored tablets. Mexican chocolate is not meant to be eaten out of hand: It has a much grainier texture than other chocolates because of the lack of cocoa butter. Abuelita and Ibarra are leading brands of Mexican chocolate that are available in the United States in Latin markets and in the baking or ethnic foods section of some supermarkets.

Churros originated in Spain (named after a Spanish sheep with long hair), but these crispy fritters, similar to crullers, quickly spread to Mexico and Argentina. In the United States, *churros* began their road to recognition in amusements parks, circuses, and malls. Today, these short, fluted sticks of fried dough have reached the masses and are even enjoyed by tourists at the Magic Kingdom at Disney World. They are fun to eat anytime but are enjoyed in Latin America particularly at breakfast, with a cup of thick hot chocolate for dunking (above). *Churros* are usually sold in streetside stalls with walk-up counters and cooked in large caldrons of sizzling oil; the whole street fills with the smell of delicious fried doughnuts. Mexican-style *churros* are sometimes filled with custard or cream.

MERENGUES

These light-as-a-cloud cookies could be named after the well-known dance of the same name because of the "shimmy" movement made when whisking the egg whites. *Merengues* are eaten all over Cuba and the Caribbean. As a tip, room-temperature whites whip better, so take them out of the fridge 20 minutes before making. Do not refrigerate or freeze these airy cookies because they soften.

MAKES 3 DOZEN

4 large egg whites, at room temperature
1/4 teaspoon cream of tartar
Juice of 1/2 lemon
1 cup sugar
1 teaspoon vanilla extract
1 teaspoon anise or almond extract

Preheat the oven to 200°F. Line 2 sheet pans with parchment paper.

In a large bowl, combine the egg whites, cream of tartar, and lemon juice. Beat with an electric mixer at medium-high speed until they just hold soft peaks. Gradually add the sugar, 1 tablespoon at a time. Add the vanilla and anise extracts. Continue to beat until the meringue is glossy and stands in stiff peaks.

Spoon the meringue into a pastry bag fitted with a large star tip. Pipe 1-inch kisses onto the pans. (Alternatively, you can drop heaping tablespoons of shapely, peaked mounds.) Bake for 1½ hours, until crisp. Turn off the oven and leave the meringues inside (with the door closed) for 1 hour to cool and completely dry out.

VARIATION: BESOS

For Chocolate *Besos* (kisses), replace the extracts with 3 tablespoons cocoa powder.

POLVORONES

Polvorones—from the Spanish word *polvo,* meaning "dust"—are so named because these melt-in-your-mouth cookies crumble easily, which is why they're often sold individually wrapped in tissue paper. When the cookies are made at home, the paper is festively colored and the package is given at weddings and other celebrations. Traditionally, *polvorones* are made with lard, but a mixture of butter and shortening also produces a wonderful cookie.

MAKES 2 DOZEN

- 1 cup chopped walnuts
- ½ cup (1 stick) unsalted butter, at room temperature
- ½ cup vegetable shortening
- 1 cup sifted confectioners' sugar, plus more for dusting
- 1 teaspoon vanilla extract
- 2 cups all-purpose flour
- Pinch of salt
- 1 teaspoon ground cinnamon, preferably Mexican *canela* (see Note, page 21)

Preheat the oven to 350°F.

Pulse the walnuts in a food processor until they're the texture of coarse meal. In a large bowl, cream the butter, shortening, 1 cup of confectioners' sugar, and vanilla with an electric mixer until fluffy, about 2 minutes. In another bowl, combine the flour, nuts, salt, and cinnamon. Gradually stir the dry ingredients into the butter mixture until blended. (If using a standing mixer, work in 3 batches to avoid flying flour; mix and scrape down the sides of the bowl with each batch.) Wrap the dough in plastic and chill in the refrigerator for 30 minutes.

Pinch off small pieces of dough and roll them into walnut-size balls. Place on parchment-lined sheet pans, about 2 inches apart. Bake for 12 to 15 minutes, until lightly browned on the bottom. (Don't overcook, or the cookies will be dry.) Roll the warm cookies in confectioners' sugar. Cool on wire racks, then roll again in the sugar.

BIZCOCHO DE **CALABAZA**

{pumpkin cake}

This Puerto Rican version of pumpkin cake is great topped with *Dulce de Leche* (page 182) or whipped cream.

SERVES 10 TO 12

2	pounds *calabaza*, peeled, cleaned, and cut into 1-inch chunks (see Note, page 43)
1¼	teaspoons salt
¾	cup whole milk
1	teaspoon vanilla extract
½	cup (1 stick) unsalted butter, at room temperature, plus 1 tablespoon, melted
1	cup sugar
2	1-ounce cones *piloncillo* or ¼ cup packed dark brown sugar and 2 tablespoons molasses (see Note, page 33)
2	large eggs
1	teaspoon grated fresh ginger
2	cups cake flour
1	teaspoon baking powder
½	teaspoon baking soda
½	teaspoon ground cinnamon, preferably Mexican *canela* (see Note, page 21)
¼	teaspoon freshly grated nutmeg
¼	teaspoon ground cloves

Boil the *calabaza* in 1 quart of water with 1 teaspoon of salt for 30 minutes, or until fork-tender. Drain and put it in a large bowl. While it's still hot, add the milk and vanilla; mash with a potato masher to blend. Set aside.

In another large bowl, cream the ½ cup butter and the sugars with an electric mixer until fluffy. Add the eggs, one at a time, beating well after each addition. Mix in the mashed *calabaza* and ginger until well blended and smooth.

Preheat the oven to 350°F. Butter a 10-inch Bundt pan with the melted butter, and dust with flour.

Combine the flour, baking powder, baking soda, remaining ¼ teaspoon salt, cinnamon, nutmeg, and cloves in another bowl. Gradually fold the dry ingredients into the *calabaza* mixture just until incorporated. Pour the batter into the prepared pan and bake for 40 to 50 minutes, until a toothpick inserted in the center comes out clean. Cool the cake in the pan for 15 minutes, then turn out onto a wire rack to cool completely.

BIZCOCHO DE **CHOCOLATE**

{chocolate cake}

This flourless chocolate cake is a fitting finale to any Mexican meal. The underlying flavors of cinnamon, almond, and orange are killer. Leftover cake is great for breakfast or for an afternoon snack.

SERVES 9

1½	cups toasted whole almonds, skinned
9	ounces Mexican or bittersweet chocolate, finely chopped (see Note, page 201)
	Finely grated zest of 1 orange
2¼	teaspoons ground cinnamon, preferably Mexican *canela* (see Note, page 21)
5	large eggs, separated, at room temperature
6	tablespoons sugar
	Pinch of salt
¼	cup heavy cream
2	tablespoons (¼ stick) unsalted butter

Preheat the oven to 325°F. Line an 8-inch square baking pan with parchment.

To prepare the cake, finely grind the almonds, 6 ounces of the chocolate, orange zest, and 2 teaspoons of the cinnamon in a food processor. In a large bowl, whisk the egg yolks with 3 tablespoons of the sugar until pale yellow and thick. Fold in the nut mixture; the batter will be very thick.

In another large bowl, combine the egg whites and salt. Using an electric mixer, beat the egg whites until frothy. Gradually add the remaining 3 tablespoons of sugar, continuing to beat until stiff peaks form.

Fold half of the beaten whites into the almond mixture to lighten it, then gently fold in the remaining half. Pour the batter into the prepared pan and smooth the top with a spatula. Bake for 40 minutes, or until a toothpick comes out clean when inserted into the cake. Let the cake cool in the pan for 10 minutes, turn out onto a wire rack, peel off the parchment paper, and cool completely.

To make the glaze, heat the cream and butter over medium-low heat until steam rises from the surface. Remove from the heat, and stir in the remaining 3 ounces chocolate and ¼ teaspoon cinnamon, until the chocolate is melted and smooth. Cool for 15 minutes, until the glaze is lukewarm. Pour the chocolate glaze over the cake, letting it drip down the sides.

{the juice stand: drinks}

HORCHATA DE ARROZ
{rice cooler}

AGUA FRESCA DE TAMARINDO
{tamarind water}

AGUA FRESCA DE PEPINO Y MELÓN
{cucumber and honeydew juice}

BATIDO
{tropical shake}

CHAMPURRADO
{chocolate atole}

PONCHE
{fruit punch}

COQUITO
{coconut eggnog}

SANGRÍA
{sangria}

MICHELADA
{spiced beer}

CORTADITO
{mexican espresso}

I REMEMBER THE FIRST TIME I saw a gringo-style

juice stand in New York City, offering a huge variety of fruit and vegetable juices freshly squeezed or pulped through machines. I couldn't believe it had taken so long for this great Latin tradition to make its way into mainstream American life, considering Americans' preoccupation with good health. *Jugoerías*—literally, juice shops—are common throughout Latin America and in the barrios. They're little shops, often with no indoor space whatsoever but just a window-counter that fronts the sidewalk; sometimes they're attached to a larger eating establishment, sometimes they're just tiny stands by the beach or park. The *jugoería* is another reflection of Latins' general lack of interest in and trust of supermarkets— we prefer not to buy half-gallon containers of orange juice from concentrate, but to get it fresh-squeezed from a cart, right in front of us, to be consumed that moment.

Jugoerías serve more than just *jugos,* which are pure juices (nothing added) of the expected fruits such as orange and grapefruit, but also mango and guava, as well as vegetables such as carrot. They also serve *aguas frescas,* which are water-based drinks mixed with homemade purées of flavors such as cantaloupe and *horchata* (rice milk, made from rice that's soaked, sugared, and puréed); the *aguas frescas* are kept in huge glass jars, and your serving is ladled out into a big drinking glass. There are also *batidos,* or milk shakes, puréed in a blender with milk, ice, sugar, and fruits such as mango, papaya, strawberry, and passionfruit. And there's more: *licuados,* which are a combination of the *agua fresca*'s water-based drink and the *batido*'s process of combining with ice. *Licuados* can have milk or alcohol, and can be whipped up in a blender or simply shaken.

The recipes in this chapter are for some of the typical *jugoería* offerings, as well as beverages that you're more likely to find in restaurants and cafés. But I decided to omit the only thing offered at yet another Latin beverage establishment, the *pulquería,* where you get one thing and one thing only: the soupy, milky, fermented, highly alcoholic (and possibly hallucinatory) extract of the agave plant, from which tequila is also made. You see, we really do have a different type of establishment for everything.

A TASTE OF PERU IN SAN FRANCISCO

On Twenty-fifth Street off Mission is El Rincón Peruano, "the Peruvian nook"—an apt name for this six-table, lunch-only place. My friend Eduardo, who's Peruvian, introduced me to El Rincón, and it immediately became a favorite. The Japanese-Peruvian chef doesn't use a set menu—he makes up a new one every day, depending on available ingredients, his mood, and the weather—for the hearty *almuerzo* (breakfast) or the lunch that's traditionally the biggest meal of the day in most of Latin America. But you can expect a few standout standards: *chupe de mariscos,* a fish stew; Peruvian-style fried rice; and the traditional *ají de gallina,* chicken stewed in the pungent mixture of *ají amarillo,* cream, and farmer's cheese. And everything goes with the fantastic condiment that sits on every table: *ají verde,* the spicy herbal purée that Peruvians love, especially on fried seafood. During the World Cup, Eduardo and I would often visit to watch the matches, washing down the delicious food with Inca Cola (Peruvian soda) and Cuzco beer, and taking in the strong South American vibe that permeates the little room.

HORCHATA DE **ARROZ**

Horchata is a refreshing drink made from soaked and strained grains, nuts, or the tuber *chufa*. It is just one of many cooling *licuados* invented to combat the hot sun of Latin America. Puerto Ricans make versions using sesame seeds, oatmeal, and sometimes barley; and the Valencia region of Spain grows *chufa* (also called earth almond and tiger nut) exclusively for making the country's famed *horchata*. Unfortunately, *chufas* are virtually extinct everywhere else on the planet; a suitable substitute for their nutty texture and taste are almonds. But *my* personal favorite has got to be rice *horchata*—I grew up gulping down glass after glass of this stuff in the summertime. A sip can really wet your whistle after a fiery meal chock-full of chiles. Soothing *horchata* is also a favorite home remedy for children with upset stomachs.

Horchata looks creamy, but does not actually contain milk. In health food stores across America and Europe, rice milk (*horchata de arroz*) is the latest dairy-free alternative to cow's milk. It contains little fat, so it is often referred to as "the drink of the gods" for its seemingly rich flavor. Sometimes tuna (the fruit of the prickly pear cactus) is puréed and swirled into *horchata*, making it pink. I like to take the extra time to simmer the rice to extract as much of the milky fluid as possible. If you're time-crunched, it's easy enough to skip that step: Just mix all the ingredients together and strain directly into a pitcher.

SERVES 4

1 cup rice

2 cinnamon sticks, preferably Mexican *canela* (see Note, page 21)

½ cup sugar

Soak the rice and cinnamon sticks in 1 quart of water overnight. Using a blender, purée the rice mixture in batches for 2 minutes to lose the grittiness. Put the puréed rice into a saucepan with the sugar and another quart of water. Simmer over medium heat for 20 minutes. Strain the rice water through a fine-mesh sieve lined with cheesecloth; twist the cloth to squeeze out all the liquid and discard the solids. Pour the liquid into a pitcher, chill in the refrigerator, and enjoy over ice.

AGUA FRESCA DE **TAMARINDO**

{tamarind water}

A common sight on the streets of Mexico are cart vendors selling an assortment of fresh cold beverages called *aguas frescas*. Typically these stands display giant glass jugs filled with a glorious array of colorful concoctions with blocks of ice floating in them. These drinks, also known as *aguas de fruta,* are mostly made from whatever fresh fruits are in season, blended with water and sugar. Some of the rainbow hues include pink (watermelon), red (jamaica, which is related to hibiscus flowers), green (melon), and amber (tamarind). These healthy drinks counterbalance the oppressive heat and spices of the region by cleansing the palate—sort of like sorbets. Tamarind water is a thirst-quenching alternative to lemonade.

SERVES 4

1 8-ounce block tamarind pulp (see Note)
3/4 cup sugar or to taste
Mint leaves, for garnish

Place the block of tamarind in a large bowl and pour a half gallon of boiling water over it. Soak the tamarind for 15 minutes to soften the pulp.

Mash the tamarind thoroughly with a fork to separate the seeds and fibers from the pulp. Strain the pulp, pressing down with a wooden spoon to squeeze out as much juice as possible; discard the solids. Mix in the sugar and cool to room temperature. Serve in tall glasses with plenty of ice, garnished with mint leaves.

TAMARIND

A large tropical tree native to India and northern Africa. The large brown pods contain seeds surrounded by a sticky sweet-sour pulp, which has a tart lemony flavor with the consistency of prunes. Tamarind (also called Indian date) can be found in Indian, Asian, and Hispanic markets in various forms. The most common is 8-ounce bricks of dried tamarind with pulp and seeds, but dried whole pods and jars of tamarind paste are also available.

From the Gulf of Mexico to the Pacific Ocean, the United States and Mexico share two thousand miles of border. The U.S. states of Texas, New Mexico, Arizona, and California are on this stretch, but the border is its own state. Within a few miles on either side of the division, this is a completely distinctive place: a mixture of Mexico and the United States, a bilingual and bicultural society in every way. People and everything else cross the border often enough that national division begins to seem abstract, even meaningless. Mexicans on the U.S. side are more in touch with their original culture and speak Spanish much more than immigrants elsewhere in the country.

This rich border culture has created a strong movement in politics and particularly the arts, with a proud, identifiable voice in literature, music, and painting. And this Chicano voice has a name for the border and much of the land north of it: *Atzlán,* an Aztec word that means "our land." The United States has spent hundreds of years wresting this land from Mexico. But throughout much of the area, Mexicans are the majority, not a minority, reclaiming the land in culture, slowly but surely.

This is where I grew up. On Saturday mornings, my dad would cross the Rio Grande for the sweet bread—*pan dulce*—that I can still taste in my mind's palate. Our housekeeper, Nico, crossed the border from her home in Juarez, Mexico, to our home in El Paso, Texas, every morning and every evening—an international commuter. She was a part of our family, much in the same way that our housekeeper in New York, Adela, was part of the family, and still is, making tamales at my mother's restaurant, Zarela. Housekeepers are not an upper-class luxury for many Mexicans, but a part of everyday middle-class life. And they do much more than just clean: They're cooks, baby-sitters, teachers, companions, trusted friends. And this is a thing we keep with us, even when we leave the border. It's one of the ways that we're making this whole country *Atzlán.*

AGUA FRESCA DE **PEPINO** Y **MELÓN**

{cucumber and honeydew juice}

The honeydew for this recipe should be almost overly ripe. The drink is a serene light green—serve in a clear pitcher and glass to grasp the full effect.

SERVES 6

2 cucumbers, preferably English, peeled and coarsely chopped
1 honeydew, peeled and coarsely chopped
12 mint leaves
Juice of 2 limes
Finely grated zest of 1 lime
¼ cup sugar

Combine the cucumbers, honeydew, and mint in a blender. Add ½ cup of water and purée until smooth. Strain the juice of seeds into a very large pitcher. Add the lime juice, zest, sugar, and 2 quarts of water. Stir to dissolve the sugar and chill thoroughly before serving.

BATIDO

{tropical shake}

This milk shake is a Puerto Rican and Cuban favorite; Palacio de Los Jugos on Flagler Street in Miami specializes in *jugos* and make great tropical-fruit *batidos*. The fruit combinations are endless—try a mixture of strawberry and kiwi or guava and pineapple—and you can even use coconut milk instead of whole and spike with a shot of rum.

SERVES 4

1 small papaya, peeled, seeded, and coarsely chopped
1 mango, peeled, seeded, and coarsely chopped
1 ripe banana, peeled and coarsely chopped
1½ cups whole milk
2 tablespoons sugar
1 cup crushed ice

Combine the fruit in a blender and purée to break everything up. Add the milk, sugar, and ice; blend until thick and frothy.

CHAMPURRADO

{chocolate atole}

Atole is a hot gruel that has been popular since the time of the Aztecs. This porridge-like drink is thickened with ground corn, or *masa*, and has the consistency of heavy cream; it's sweetened with sugar and flavored with cinnamon, fruit, almonds, or chocolate. Chocolate *atole*, called *champurrado*, is the best kind, like thick hot chocolate that warms you up from the inside out. *Atole* is a natural accompaniment for *chepas* (sweet tamales) or kings' cake (*rosca de reyes*, a type of pound cake) but is also very filling and satisfying on its own, and is renowned for pacifying the palate after a spicy meal. A *molinillo* is a small wooden stick with rings and grooves that is used to froth the chocolate drink and create a cap of foam on top. It is believed that the person making the *champurrado* creates friction by rubbing the stick back and forth and thus transfers their energy into the cup.

SERVES 4

½ cup *masa harina* (see Note, page 77)

1 cinnamon stick, preferably Mexican *canela* (see Note, page 21)

3 cups whole milk

3 ounces Mexican or dark chocolate, grated (see Note, page 201)

Combine the *masa harina* with 2 cups of water in a large saucepan and place over medium heat. Add the cinnamon and bring to a boil. Simmer for 10 minutes, stirring constantly, until the mixture thickens.

In another saucepan, combine the milk and chocolate and place over medium heat. Simmer and stir until the chocolate has completely melted, about 10 minutes. Pour the chocolate milk into the *masa* mixture, stirring until well incorporated. Remove the cinnamon stick. With a *molinillo* or whisk, whip to froth the surface. Serve hot in mugs, spooning some of the foam on top of each cup.

PONCHE

This sweet-and-sour fruit punch is a holiday favorite in Mexico, and I feature it on the menu at Paladar for the entire month of December. Different fruits can be used at your discretion, but be sure to include a mixture of tart dried and fresh fruits for a well-rounded flavor. Sometimes I add some cloves or allspice along with the cinnamon to make it more like a hot toddy.

SERVES 12

- 4 Golden Delicious apples, cored and cut in wedges
- ½ pound crab apples, quartered
- 1 medium pineapple, peeled, cored, and cut into large chunks
- 1 pound guavas, peeled, seeded, and quartered
- ½ cup pitted prunes
- ¾ cup raisins
- 1 cup sugar
- 3 4-inch pieces sugarcane, cut into strips (optional)
- 4 cinnamon sticks, preferably Mexican *canela* (see Note, page 21)
- 8 whole juniper berries
- 1 cup tequila

In a large pot, combine the fruit, sugar, sugarcane, cinnamon, juniper berries, and 3 quarts of water. Bring to a boil, then lower the heat and simmer for 1 hour, covered, to cook down the fruit, stirring occasionally. Put a shot (or two) of tequila into each mug and ladle the hot *ponché* into the cups.

COQUITO

{coconut eggnog}

Coconut eggnog, a national treasure of Puerto Rico, is the quintessential holiday drink. Homemade *coquito* is served to visitors throughout the extended Christmas holidays, which are celebrated in Puerto Rico and throughout much of the Caribbean from early December through mid-January, and it is also a frequent Christmas present in a "from our home to your home" way. I know it may sound strange, but I don't put egg yolks in this eggnog. I find it to be too heavy, and people are a little squeamish about drinking raw egg yolks. Serve it out of a coconut shell if you want to get extra fancy. With a whole bottle of rum in the recipe . . . welcome to a Latin party!

SERVES 12
MAKES APPROXIMATELY 2 1/2 QUARTS

- 3 cinnamon sticks, preferably Mexican *canela* (see Note, page 21)
- 1/4 teaspoon whole cloves
- 1 1-inch piece fresh ginger, halved and smashed
- 2 15-ounce cans cream of coconut
- 2 12-ounce cans evaporated milk
- 1 teaspoon vanilla extract
- 1 1-liter bottle white rum
  Freshly grated nutmeg, for garnish

In a small saucepan, combine the cinnamon, cloves, and ginger with 2 cups of water. Simmer for 5 minutes to reduce the liquid to 1 cup; the water should be tinted and smell fragrant. Fish out the spices and let cool to room temperature.

Combine the cream of coconut, evaporated milk, and vanilla in a blender. Purée for a full minute until completely smooth. Pour the cream into a container and stir in the spiced water and rum. Chill really well. Serve in small glasses dusted with nutmeg.

SANGRÍA

{sangria}

Sangre means "blood" in Spanish, hence the name of this time-honored party drink. You can really use any type of wine and fruit; it's all good.

SERVES 12

- 2 750-ml bottles dry red wine, such as Rioja
- 1 cup brandy
- ½ cup orange juice
- ½ cup superfine sugar
- 2 lemons, unpeeled and sliced
- 2 oranges, unpeeled and sliced
- 1 medium pineapple, peeled, cored, and cut into large chunks
- 1 honeydew melon, peeled and cut into chunks
- 1 star fruit, sliced
- 1 liter club soda

Combine the wine, brandy, orange juice, and sugar in a large pitcher. Stir to dissolve the sugar. Mix in the fruit. Chill in the refrigerator for at least 4 hours or up to overnight. Add the club soda just before serving. Pour into glasses filled with ice.

MICHELADA

This unique Mexican drink is served in *taquerías* with pilsner or lager–style beers.

SERVES 4

1 chile de árbol, stemmed and seeded (see Note, page 231)
¼ cup coarse salt
2 limes, halved
4 teaspoons Tampico hot sauce or Tabasco
4 cans or bottles of Dos Equis or Sol beer

In a dry cast-iron skillet, toast the chile over medium-low heat for 2 minutes, until fragrant; turn it and shake the pan so it doesn't scorch. Put the chile in a clean coffee grinder or spice mill and grind to a powder. Combine the chile powder with the salt and spread it out on a small plate.

Coat the rim of each beer glass with a little lime to moisten. Press the glass into the chile-salt to coat the rim. Put 1 teaspoon of hot sauce in the glass, followed by a good squeeze of lime. Pour the beer in the glass and enjoy!

CORTADITO

Latinos are very particular about their coffee—strong and sweet is the rule, and this is both. Think of it as espresso with a kick. Milk is very optional.

SERVES 4

2 teaspoons finely ground Espresso coffee beans
2 teaspoons sugar
1 teaspoon water
12 ounces hot brewed espresso coffee

Combine the coffee granules, sugar, and water in a small bowl. Whisk with a fork to make a paste. Divide the paste among 4 coffee cups and pour the hot espresso over each. Sip and enjoy.

Chocolate is a mixture of sugar and ground cocoa beans, which are the seeds of the tropical cacao tree—called *cacahuatl* by the Aztecs. Cocoa was once used as currency in Mexico, and consumed only by the very rich; Aztec workers were once paid twenty cacao beans for a month's work. When Christopher Columbus arrived in the Aztec land in 1502, he was offered gifts that included cocoa. Decades later, Cortés brought the first shipment to Europe.

Mexican chocolate is different from that in Europe or the United States. The style of roasting, sugaring, and grinding creates a flavor that's less sweet, more earthy and mineral-like, with a coarser, more granular texture. And sweet milk chocolate is not common—Mexican chocolate is usually bitter or semisweet. Throughout Mexico, but particularly in the beautiful colonial city of Oaxaca, you'll find chocolate shops that create mixtures to taste, and you can have one custom-produced to your desired degree of sweetness, with additions like almonds (for *almendrado*) and almost always cinnamon; you take away a little bag of the freshly ground powder.

The differences among Mexican chocolate reflects different uses. Although the chocolate is eaten as candy, it is often used to make drinks called *champurrado* (made from corn) and *atole,* as well as *chocolate caliente*—hot chocolate that's frothed by twisting a stick (called a *violinillo*) in the mixture and is made with milk, not water. But perhaps most notable are chocolate's uses in savory dishes, especially the mole sauces that often include dozens of ingredients including chiles, spices, vegetables, ground bread, and chocolate. You may be tentative about eating chicken in a thick, rich *mole poblano,* but the barely sweetened chocolate isn't sweeter than a ripe tomato, and imparts a rich earthiness that has nothing to do with a Hershey's bar.

Similarly, cinnamon is not just a flavoring for sweet desserts like flan—it too can be found in some *moles.* Mexican cinnamon, called *canela,* is longer, flatter, and generally not curled into a tight cylinder like the American version. Its flavor is more intense, but less medicinal and astringent.

As with many cooking ingredients, there can be a world of difference among items that share the same name. The next time you're shopping, try to score a tablet of Mexican chocolate, or a tin of *canela.* I'm not saying they're better—although I think they are—just that they're different. In a good way.

QUESADILLA SUIZA

{essential recipes}